Backyard Builder's Bonanza

Percy W. Blandford

TAB TAB BOOKS
Blue Ridge Summit, PA

FIRST EDITION
THIRD PRINTING

© 1989 by **TAB Books**.
TAB Books is a division of McGraw-Hill, Inc.

Library of Congress Cataloging-in-Publication Data

Blandford, Percy W.
    Backyard builder's bonanza / by Percy W. Blandford.
       p.   cm.
    Includes index.
    ISBN 0-8306-1974-7   ISBN 0-8306-3174-7 (pbk.)
    1. Garden structures—Design and construction—Amateurs' manuals.
  I. Title.
  TH4961.B57 1989
  684.1′8—dc20   89-4558
                                                       CIP

TAB Books offers software for sale. For information and a catalog, please contact
TAB Software Department, Blue Ridge Summit, PA 17294-0850.

Acquisitions Editor: Kimberly Tabor
Manuscript Editor: Stephen Moro
Production: Katherine G. Brown

Contents

Introduction

A garden is primarily a place where you hope things will grow. You might be mainly interested in producing vegetables and fruit. Your inclinations might be more toward flowers and shrubs. You might have enough land to divide into vegetable plots, formal gardens, and informal areas. There could be a large expanse of lawn with borders of flowers, bushes, and trees. At the other extreme, you might have little more than a few potted plants and a window box.

Almost certainly you will have to fence your garden or yard and provide gates. There might have to be terraces. Climbing plants will need supports of varying complexity. Coupled with all this could be a deck to give balance to the garden layout.

Although you might not think you have much ability in working wood or metal, a large number of useful projects can be completed with the minimum of skill and very few hand tools.

If you are more of a workshop enthusiast with extensive equipment, you can make almost all the items you need to be a successful gardener. Obviously, there are a few things that cannot be made with the usual home-shop facilities, but you can satisfy nearly all your gardening needs with things you make yourself.

And this is what this book is all about. May you enjoy the combination of successful gardening and satisfaction in your craftsmanship.

Note: Unless otherwise indicated, sizes are in inches and they are quoted in descending order of dimensions: length, width, and thickness. It is common to allow a little extra on lengths when obtaining wood.

1
CHAPTER

Craftsmanship

The combination of crafts enthusiast and gardener in one person opens up many interesting possibilities. Taken to extremes, you could spend all your time in the shop making things and have no time left to go outside and use them. That could happen if you tried to make all the projects in this book; you have to be selective.

Few of the products require a high degree of skill or very elaborate facilities. What you choose to make depends on your needs, inclinations, shop equipment, and your ability to make the best use of what you have. Most beginner craftsmen can tackle basic woodworking. Because many outdoor wood projects are made without cut joints, construction is very easy and can be done with few hand tools. Power tools will help by lessening labor and sometimes increasing accuracy.

It is the working of metal that will worry some readers. A few enthusiastic woodworkers have a prejudice against working in metal. If you have some skill at woodwork, basic metalwork should come naturally. For most projects involving metal, you only have to saw, file, drill, and bend. A substantial metal vise is valuable, but the other tools needed are simple and you might have them already.

Whether or not to tackle some of the more advanced projects involving metal depends on your facilities for joining parts. If you have welding equipment, almost anything is possible. Without it you can still make strong joints by *brazing*— using the flame of a propane torch. Easier, although less strong, is soldering. A combination of rivets with brazing can provide good tool strength.

You can make things that pivot on bolts or rivets and have only a simple action, but if the device has rotating parts as well you will almost certainly need a metalworking lathe. This, and the fact that most machines need special parts not always easy to obtain, makes the production of garden machines unsuitable for the majority of metalworking gardeners.

Although most readers will not have a metalworking lathe, more will be able to turn wood. Wood turning is not essential—you can produce acceptable parts without a lathe—but turned parts, where appropriate, give the tool or equipment a better appearance. This is particularly so with handles. An attraction for the user of woodturning lathe is that handles and other parts can be made to exactly fit their needs. This is not always so with some manufacturers that use stock handles for a variety of the tools they sell.

An attraction of making your own outdoor equipment is that you are dealing with one-off projects, made to exactly fit a need. A deck will be exactly the size you want it. A tool shed can fit a space exactly. It can accommodate equipment measured to fit.

Overall you have the satisfaction of knowing that the complete concept is under your control. When laying out the whole or part of your property, you can make things to suit and you suddenly will not find that a purchased seat, shed, gate, or other item cannot be made to fit. You make it and it will fit.

Very low on the list of priorities for a craftsman gardener is economy. Advantages of making things to exactly suit their purpose and the sheer satisfaction of saying, "I made that," outweigh considerations of cost. Usually, of course, the homemade tool is less expensive than the purchased equivalent (if there is one), that is, assuming you are not allowing yourself a wage. Making individual tools for sale would involve a high selling price if the scheme is to be viable. With larger projects, there might be no mass-produced item to compare. You might find a prefabricated tool shed or seat to compare, but a fence, gate, arch or other item fitted to its surroundings will not be like anything you could buy. Economically you will have a very good deal compared with paying some-one else to do the job.

Planning is important. Do not rush into making things, particularly large projects, and then find they will not fit or do not match their surroundings. It is helpful to draw a plan of the garden and yard—with the house and other fixtures shown on it—even if your property has a simple square outline. If the drawing is to scale and you draw additions to scale or cut their outlines to shape on loose paper to move around, you will avoid most mistakes. Even things like widths of paths or gates in relation to wheel tracks of carts to be used need advanced planning. If you are making a shed or tool locker, measure the contents first or you will feel silly having to shorten a handle to get it in.

You might already have some garden tools and equipment. Do these things function as they should? Before rushing into making new tools, you might be able to think of ways of altering or improving existing tools. Even if you decide to make replacements, there might be old parts you can recycle. Handles of discarded tools can be used again. Any old mild steel strip or rod will often find a new use. Pieces of tool steel are worth having even if they have not been tools. Springs are tool steel. Sheet mild steel can be cut from many discarded domestic appliances.

An advantage of wood that has already been used is that it can be assumed to be well seasoned. Obviously, if there are signs of rot or worm holes, you will not want to use the wood again, but much useful wood can be obtained from old furniture, crates, and similar things.

In a garden you will probably want to make bins and containers to hold soil or store crops. Although new wood can be used, an assembly of recycled wood can be just as effective. Even plywood with non-waterproof glue might last several months in dry weather. Another advantage of old wood is that its appearance will probably blend into its surroundings.

If you are an enthusiastic gardener but you live in an area where, for many months of the winter, you cannot work outside, making tools and equipment—prefabricating parts of sheds, seats, fences and other large projects—can keep your gardening interest alive. When you can work outside again, it will not take long to install your new work and then get on with the serious business of sowing, planting, and all the activities your garden will demand of you.

2
CHAPTER

Wood and Joints

Most amateur craftsmen make things from wood. It is assumed that you have some familiarity with wood and the basic techniques of working it with hand and power tools. Wood is a good choice for making a great many things, and it has many applications in equipment for the garden and yard.

Almost any wood has possibilities. You can buy lumber, you can recycle wood that has been used in some other construction, or you can cut and convert wood growing on your own land.

Broadly, woods are divided into *hardwoods* and *softwoods*. The names are not strictly true definitions as the differences are botanical rather than descriptions of relative hardness. The majority of hardwoods are harder than most softwoods. The softwoods available are mostly firs, spruces, and pines. Some softwoods are not durable, but if they are resinous they have a longer life. Most hardwoods, such as oak, can be assumed to be much longer-lasting. Hardwoods tend to be heavy. For tools where lightness is important, it would be advisable to choose softwood and accept the fact that it will not last as long. Softwood can be protected with paint and preservative and by storing it in a place when not in use.

Wood straight from the tree contains a considerable amount of moisture in the form of sap. There is less sap if the tree is felled in the winter, but there is still more than can be accepted for anything except rough construction. If you are planning rustic work where stability of the wood is not important, you can go ahead with it straight away. For anything else, the wood should be dried to a small moisture content through the process called *seasoning*. If wood is not seasoned, it will shrink and warp after being built into something, and it might develop lengthwise shakes (cracks).

Natural seasoning is done by stacking boards in a sheltered place, but where air can circulate, and then leaving them for some time. (One year for each inch of thickness is appropriate.) Commercially there are faster methods of seasoning. Lumber bought from a regular supplier should be correctly seasoned. Even then it is a good idea to buy well ahead of your needs and keep the wood for perhaps two months before using it. Then you can see if the wood will retain its shape and size.

Softwoods are sold in a standard sections so it is advisable to plan projects to suit them. Everyone knows about 2 × 4s, but there are many others sizes. With hardwoods it is advisable to check what sections your supplier has, rather than present him with a cutting list of different sections. Otherwise he will charge you extra. Of course, if you have your own power saw of sufficient capacity, you could buy economical larger sections and cut them down yourself.

Wood is typically sold in the size it is quoted as sawn. Although 2 inches × 4 inches might be the true sawn size, a planed 2 × 4 will actually be 1⅞ inch × 3⅞ inch (or less), and you should allow for that in your projects. There are several outdoor projects that can be made with wood that has not been planed, but an advantage of buying planed wood is that you are better able to see any flaws quickly rather than discover them later.

Natural wood, either round as it comes from the tree or just split down the middle, has many uses in the garden for making fences, arches, and similar things. Even smaller plant pot containers or other more compact constructions can be made with small pieces of poles or branches. You must first decide whether to use the wood with its bark on or to strip it off first. Most fir, spruce, and similar softwoods tend to shed their bark as they dry and shrink. What might look attractive when first constructed could eventually take on an untidy appearance where some bark is retained and other has fallen off. That wood is better stripped of its bark before making the wood into a project.

Some woods have bark that is very securely held. You could decide to leave it, but in general it is better to remove bark. Insects and other pests tend to gather between bark and wood. It is better for the life of the wood, and possibly for things growing nearby, to strip the poles or branches down to the wood.

Plywood has many uses in outdoor constructions; make sure you get the type bonded with a waterproof glue, which is described as *exterior* or *marine* grade. The latter is more expensive and not usually necessary. Veneers mainly affect appearance. For something like a compost container, the lowest veneer category might be just as useful as the more costly high-quality plywood. If your project is a piece of patio furniture, the better-looking, high-grade plywood would be preferable.

Hardboard is not suitable for outdoor use. Even the oil-tempered type will not stand up to weather for long. Particleboard and some of the other manufactured boards might have exterior uses, but check what the manufacturer says about specific grades. In general, you are more likely to be satisfied with solid wood and the appropriate plywood for exterior work.

Not so long ago, joints in exterior woodwork required mechanical fasteners because there were no glues that would stand up to moist conditions indefinitely. Otherwise, there had to be wedges or interlocking joints. All of these techniques are still used, but there are modern, fully waterproof glues that will make secure joints unaided or to complement mechanical fasteners. Some of these glues are in two parts to be mixed before use or applied separately to the surfaces before bringing them together. Others are one-part glues. Unfortunately, trade names do not always give you a clue to the chemical content. If the glue is a two-part product or described as suitable for boats, it should be fully waterproof and strong enough.

NAILS

Many wood things for use in the garden or yard are nailed together, which is quite satisfactory for most assemblies. Usually there is not much to worry about, providing you use sufficient nails of sufficient length and you take care to hit the nail and not your own project!

Common nails are made from round wire. These and the similar "box" nails are suitable for most garden carpentry. They are made of mild steel (which will rust), so it is advisable to buy them protected with zinc or other coating. Lengths usually available are from 1 inch to 6 inches, with increases in diameter to suit. They are sold by penny sizes, from 2d for a 1-inch nail through 6d for a 2-inch nail, and 20d for a 4-inch nail to 60d for a 6-inch nail.

If you are joining two pieces of wood, it is the amount of nail in the lower piece that provides strength. Therefore, you must choose a nail that will have enough penetration. How much penetration needed is more a matter of experience than a matter of rule, but you need a greater length in softwood than in hardwood and more in end grain than in side grain.

For many assemblies you can drive nails without drilling, but it might help you to drill the top piece to the same size as the nail diameter. This makes for easier driving and reduces any tendency to split the top piece; moreover, it is advisable near an edge—even if you drive without drilling further along.

You can increase the strength of a nailed joint by dovetail nailing (Fig. 2-1A), with alternate nails sloping opposite ways. It also increases strength in the joint to put end nails closer together (Fig. 2-1B).

With thin wood you might only be able to get sufficient strength by taking a nail through and clenching its point. This will also provide a pivot if two parts have to move on each other. An example is a trellis that will fold when not required to be opened out. The best way to clench is to drive the nail through, with enough point projecting (Fig. 2-1C), and then curve the point over a spike while the other side is supported on an iron block (Fig. 2-1D). While still supporting the other side, bury the point diagonal to the grain (Fig. 2-1E), rather than along the grain (which might start a split).

SCREWS

Screws can be described as *wood screws* to distinguish them from *metal-thread screws*, that are used with nuts. Screws provide a more positive fastening than nails, with joints that are pulled closer and stronger. It is also easier to withdraw a screw with less risk of damage to the wood. Screwed construction is considered superior to nailing and is preferred for better work.

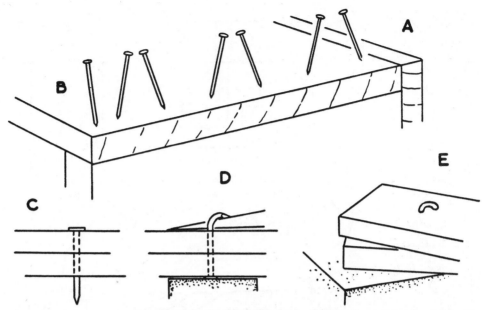

Fig. 2-1. The strength of a nailed joint is increased if nails are driven dovetail fashion. With thin wood, a nail will go through and can be clenched.

There are several types of screws, but for most purposes flat-headed ones are appropriate (Fig. 2-2A). Round-head screws are the only other type you are likely to need (Fig. 2-2B). The types with slotted heads for a common screwdriver are all you need, but other types with socket heads are really intended for quantity production and require special screwdrivers.

Screws are described by their length from the surface of the wood and are obtainable in several gauge thicknesses for each length. In small sizes, there are single-gauge number differences, but in lengths from about 1½ inches up, your supplier will probably only have even-number gauge sizes. Table 2-1 shows the most-used screw sizes.

Common screws made from mild steel can be bought protected from rust by various platings. They might be made of brass, which has a good resistance to moisture, one of several other metals that usually are more costly but also have a good resistance to corrosion.

The threaded part of a screw is about two-thirds of its length, and it is the pull of this in the lower piece of wood that draws the top piece tightly down. There is nothing to be gained by having the screw a tight fit in the top piece.

There should be a clearance hole for the shank of the screw in the top piece (Fig. 2-2C). If that wood is thin and part of the parallel shank enters the lower piece, you could also take the clearance-size drill a little farther. Otherwise, the plain shank forcing its way there may lift fibers on the surface and interfere with the joint pulling tight. With a small-diameter screw in softwood, you can start

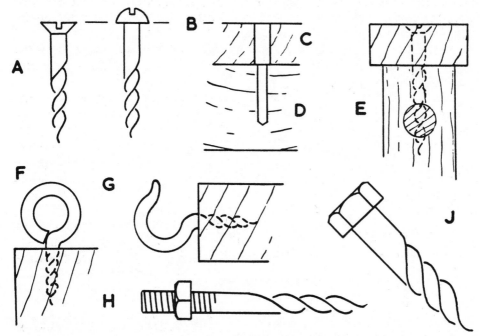

Fig. 2-2. Wood screws need holes (A-D) and can be strengthened in end grain with a dowel (E). Other parts can have screw ends (F-J).

Length (inches)	Gauge Sizes Available
1	6, 8, 10
1¼	8, 10, 12
1½	8, 10, 12
2	8, 10, 12, 14
2½	10, 12, 14
3	14, 16, 18
4	16, 18, 20

Table 2-1. Common Screw Sizes.

the screw in the lower piece with a tap from a hammer and let it cut its own way in as you turn it. In most cases, it is better to drill an undersize hole in the lower piece (Fig. 2-2D). In softwood, it need not be as large, nor go as far, as a hole in hardwood.

With many woods, a flat head will pull itself in flush with the surface. With harder wood, you can use a countersink bit to prepare the hole. Even then, it is advisable to only partly countersink to allow for some pulling in. Round heads are more often used to hold metal to wood, but otherwise it is worthwhile putting a washer under the head to spread the load and increase pressure.

Screws are generally stronger than nails so they can be more widely spaced, but there should still be a good penetration of the lower wood and a greater length allowed in end grain. Screws can be installed closer to an edge. For an assembly like a box corner, you could use a screw for strength near the open top, while nails are used in the joint further down.

The grip in end grain is much less than in cross grain, particularly in some softwoods, and this can be improved by putting a dowel across so that the screw goes through its cross grain (Fig. 2-2E).

Wood screw ends are provided in some other applications. Screw eyes (Fig. 2-2F) have uses in many outdoor projects such as hanging containers. There are several sizes and forms of screw hooks (Fig. 2-2G) that have obvious applications. Less obvious is the hanger screw or bolt (Fig. 2-2H). This is used where you want to drive a wood screw—usually because you cannot take a bolt right through—and then attach a metal part. To drive a hanger bolt, tighten two nuts on it against each other, and then use a wrench on the top nut to turn the screw into a hole in the wood. Release the nuts by using two wrenches.

Very large and thick screws would be very difficult to turn tight with an ordinary screwdriver. Therefore, lag screws or coach screws (Fig. 2-2J) have heads to take wrenches. They must be started by hammering into the top of an undersize hole.

JOINTS

For much exterior woodwork, it will be sufficient to put one piece of wood over another and either nail or screw it there. In some constructions, such as seats and tables, the joints will have to be more like those for interior furniture. Even then, there are some variations advisable to suit the exterior situation.

If you want to positively locate one part over another, even if the fastening is to be a nail or screw, it is a help to notch one of the pieces (Fig. 2-3A). Notch both pieces if accuracy of location is needed both ways. This will help to retain symmetry even with rustic poles. The notches can be quite shallow.

If parts have to cross at the same level, whether square to each other or not, you must cut a halving joint (Fig. 2-3B). This weakens the wood. If you can cross without bringing surfaces to the same level, the notches can be shallower and the wood stronger.

Dowel construction is possible for some things, but you are then dependent upon only glue. It is better to build in some mechanical strength. That is more easily done with mortise and tenon joints. If the ordinary mortise and tenon joint has the tenon right through (Fig. 2-3C), there can be one or two saw cuts across the tenon end and wedges can be driven in (Fig. 2-3D). Do this with the wedges in the direction that expands the wood of the tenon toward the end grain of the mortised part.

A good way of coupling mechanical and glued strength is to draw-pin a mortise-and-tenon joint. For large seats and similar things, where it would be difficult to use clamps, draw-pinning pulls joints together. Cut a mortise-and-tenon joint, and then drill across the mortised part, either central or toward the side where the tenon shoulder will come. In the tenon, mark and drill a similar hole, but slightly toward the shoulder (Fig. 2-3E). How far you move this depends

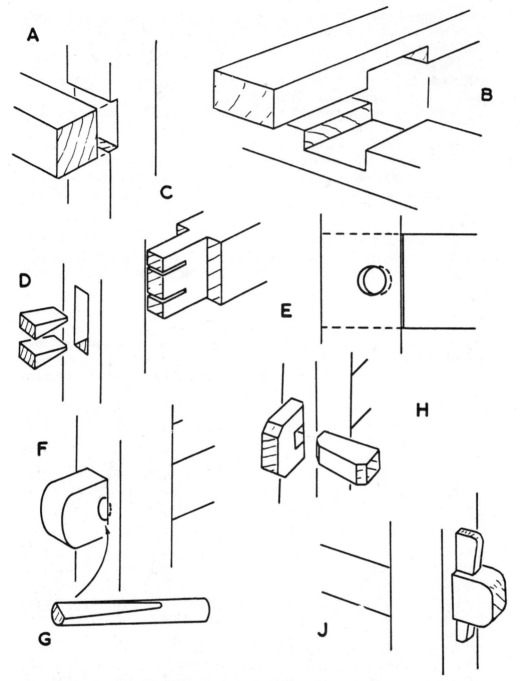

Fig. 2-3. Parts can be notched together (A,B) or tenoned with wedges (D-J).

on the wood, but ⅛ inch is probably right for a ½-inch hole. Taper the end of a dowel rod longer than the thickness of the wood. Glue the parts and fit them together. Drive in the tapered dowel to pull the joint tight, and then cut off the extending tapered and top parts.

Another way to tighten a mortise-and-tenon joint is with external wedges through what are called *tusk tenons*. This method can also serve as decoration. In its simplest form, let the end of the tenon extend and drill a hole across that will have its edge below the surface of the other part (Fig. 2-3F). Plane a taper on the side of a dowel that fits the hole in order to make a wedge (Fig. 2-3G), and drive that through the hole with the flat surfaces together. This pulls the tenon tighter into its mortise. The end of the tenon can be shaped and the dowel cut so it projects evenly after driving.

A wedge with a rectangular section might look better than a tapered dowel. The important thing is to cut the slot for the wedge so its inner edge is below the surface of the mortised part. This way the wedge forces outwards against the wood of the tenon. The slot should taper to match the wedge (Fig. 2-3H), which can have decorated ends.

It may be better in some constructions to have the wedge the other way through the tenon (Fig. 2-3J). In all of the these wedged tenons, there is a considerable thrust on the end grain. It is advisable to only use the method on compact hardwoods and then to allow adequate wood outside the slot.

Variations on these and other joints are described in this book. For most exterior woodwork, simpler joints are preferable to some of the more complicated ones appropriate to indoor constructions.

EDGE JOINTS

For some outdoor projects you will need to join pieces of wood to make up sufficient width. Where a wide board is available it is usually preferable, but there may be a risk of warping and that is often counteracted by different grain patterns in several boards joined to make up a comparable width. If you are buying wood, the wide pieces might be disproportionately more costly due to their rarity.

Gluing is the obvious way to join boards edge to edge, and modern waterproof glues should be just as successful outdoors as indoors, providing the wood has been seasoned to only a small moisture content. No glue can be very effective on wood containing an excess of water. If the wood is unsuitable for gluing, it is still possible to make a mechanical joint that will be satisfactory in many outdoor situations. Even with simple glued joints, there might be a problem in an assembly that has to stand up to all the rigors of year-round exposure. The glue line might hold, but wood fibers nearby might fail. Therefore, it would be advisable to do more than merely glue surface to surface.

For many assemblies, strips can be joined with cleats or battens across at the back or underneath (Fig. 2-4A). These pieces can be just nailed or screwed. If you are putting something together fairly wide that might have to withstand rain and sunlight, there ought to be an allowance for expansion and contraction. This

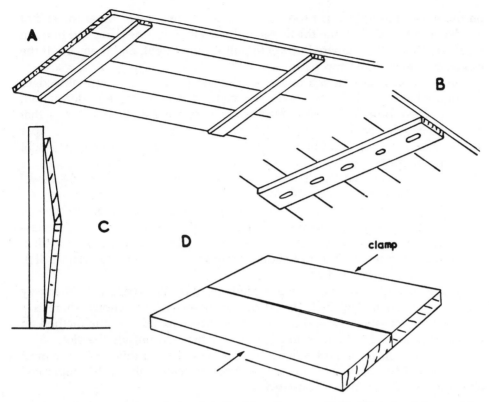

Fig. 2-4. A wide top can have the boards held with strips across (A,B). Edges for gluing must be checked square (C), and a slight hollow helps in clamping tightly (D).

will apply to a door or tabletop, possibly 30 inches wide, when a ¼-inch alteration in total width could be expected at different seasons.

The variations can be taken care of by slot screwing. If equal expansion has to be allowed for, use round holes for central screws, but put those further out in slots (Fig. 2-4B) up to ¼ inch long or more toward the outside. If it is an assembly where one side should remain unaltered, put screws at that side in round holes and have the others in slots getting progressively longer toward the other side.

If dry wood is to be glued edge to edge, plane both edges straight and try them together to see that they will not finish out of true on the surfaces (Fig. 2-4C). Trouble comes with ends of joints opening. This can be avoided by making the meeting surfaces very slightly hollow in the length, and then a central bar clamp can be used to close the joint and the ends will be forced tighter than the center (Fig. 2-4D). If there have to be several edge joints to make up a width, it is wiser to make them one at a time. This will reduce the risk of the boards buckling out of true while clamping.

If increased strength is wanted in an end joint, dowels can be included. How many and their spacing depend on circumstances. For example, a joint in a tabletop of 1-inch boards might have ⅜-inch dowels at 6-inch intervals. Care is

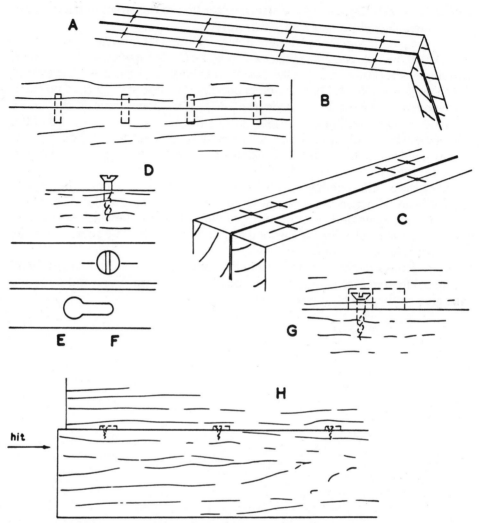

Fig. 2-5. Edge joints can be doweled (A,B) or held with secret slot screws (D-H).

needed in marking out. Put the planed edges together and mark across, and then gauge from what will be the top surfaces (Fig. 2-5A). Drill slightly too deep. Dowels going 1 inch into each piece should be sufficient (Fig. 2-5B). Taper the ends of the dowels so they will enter easily. A saw cut along each dowel is worthwhile because it lets air and surplus glue escape as the joint is clamped.

Secret slot screwing is a good way of strengthening a joint and pulling it together. This is just as suitable for outdoor as indoor woodwork. It is intended for use with glue, but even without glue it will lock edges together in addition to battens or in place of them. The method uses screws in one edge, with their heads projecting into slots in the other piece. Careful marking out is essential.

For boards about 1 inch thick, suitable fasteners are steel screws 1 inch by 8 (or 10 gauge). If you are using hardwood, choose thicker screws because they have to resist bending. Space the screws according to the strength needed, but 6-inch intervals will probably be satisfactory.

Put the boards together and mark hole positions as if for using dowels, and then mark more hole centers ½ inch away (Fig. 2-5C). Drive screws into the board with single-hole positions, going far enough in to bury the threads and leave about ¼ inch projecting (Fig. 2-5D). In the other board, drill holes, at the second position, large enough to clear the screw heads (Fig. 2-5E). At the points opposite the screws in the other board, drill holes of a size to clear the neck of the screws. All of the holes should be slightly deeper than the projection of the screws. Make slots from the small holes into the larger ones. Some of the waste can be drilled away and the slots trued with a chisel (Fig. 2-5F).

Bring the boards together with the screw heads in the large holes (Fig. 2-5G). Hit one board along so the screw head cuts its way along the slot (Fig. 2-5H). Knock it back again and coat the surfaces with glue. Tighten each screw one-quarter of a turn and assemble the joint again. As you drive one board along the other, the joint should pull very tight.

Brass screws might seem more suited to outdoor use, but they might bend during tightening, except in very soft wood. The screws are buried and protected with glue so there is little risk of steel rusting.

3
CHAPTER

Metal

Basic metalwork is as interesting and no more difficult than woodworking.

Many tools and equipment for the garden and yard combine wood and metal. This combination offers some interesting work, and probably a greater satisfaction to the maker than something in wood or metal alone. A knowledge of metals and alloys helps in selecting suitable material and knowing about the effects of heat treatments give you scope for interesting constructions.

IRON AND STEEL

Most tools for garden and farm have their principal parts made of what is loosely termed "iron." That is a convenient general term, but it is not strictly correct any more than talking of a "tin" roof. Tin is a valuable metal and a roof made of it would be very expensive. The roofing material is really iron coated with zinc. This combination has a good resistance to corrosion. Tin is used as a very thin protective coating on iron for cans and other things because it is safe in contact with foodstuffs. Tin is not used on roofs.

Pure—or almost pure—iron is rare today. It is sought after by blacksmiths for the ease with which it can be worked, but now they have to be satisfied, usually, with mild steel. Cast iron is a form of iron, often with many impurities, that can be melted and poured into a mold. It is of use when a part has to be cast, but it is unsuitable for working in bar and strip and cannot be made into sheets. As the heat needed to melt iron to be cast is greater than anyone except a specialist worker would have, cast iron (except as ready-made parts) is of no interest to the maker of tools to be used on the land.

Steel is iron containing a proportion of carbon (which alters iron's characteristics). It is sometimes spoken of as an alloy, a mixture of metals, but as carbon is not a metal the term is not strictly correct. A small amount of carbon in iron does not have much effect on it. Such *mild steel* is usually inferred today when "iron" is used. Mild steel is not as ductile, or moldable, as pure iron, but it can still be bent and shaped or forged to a sufficient degree. Steel is more prone to rust than pure iron.

Rust is oxidation of the surface due to the effect of moisture in the atmosphere. The corrosion is a layer of ferrous (iron) oxide. On pure iron, the first corrosion is slight and this forms a skin that restricts further corrosion. On steel, corrosion will go on progressively if unchecked by protective coatings. This could be a coating of other metal with a good resistance to corrosion, painting, or occasional wiping with oil or grease (which is the most usual treatment for outdoor tools).

Anything that does not have to cut can be satisfactorily made with mild steel, sometimes termed *low-carbon steel*. With an increased amount of carbon, the steel will accept heat treatment so that it can be hardened and tempered (the dual treatment for giving it the required hardness) or annealed (which brings it to its softest state). This is *high-carbon* or *tool steel*. Straightforward tool steel made into many tools can be heat treated satisfactorily with the facilities available to most craftsmen or the operators of small shops. There might not be the precision that is available for heat treating at a large manufacturing plant, but simple methods and approximate temperatures should give a satisfactory result.

Today there are a large number of steels with other metals alloyed to give special characteristics, including stainless and nonmagnetic. Unfortunately, these steels require careful temperature control when heat treating. Therefore, they are unsuitable for most makers of individual tools. When something harder than mild steel is required, the choice should be straight tool steel.

For practical purposes nothing you do to it will affect the characteristics of mild steel enough to notice. It can be hammered, bent, drilled, machined and forged to different shapes. Then its characteristics will still be the same.

HARDENING

If you heat tool steel to redness and cool it rapidly in water, it will be hardened. It is then as hard as it can be, but unfortunately it is also brittle. If it is given a cutting edge, it will crack or splinter if you try to use it. If you dropped the tool it might break. Metal-cutting files are left fully hard, or almost so, but this state would be unsuitable for other tools.

ANNEALING

If you heat tool steel to redness and let it cool extremely slowly, it will be annealed to the softest state it can be. New tool steel might be already fully annealed and described so by the makers. If you want to anneal tool steel yourself, the best way is to heat it in a fire and leave it to cool overnight with the fire. If you heat it with a blow-lamp flame, surround it with coke or other fuel, so that is heated as well, and then leave it all to cool. Annealing is important if you want to machine or drill the steel. In any state but not fully annealed, you would blunt the drill and probably not make a hole. The drill is also tool steel; it cannot be expected to cut through something as hard as itself. Today, drills are usually alloyed with other metals to give increased toughness, but they still cannot cut through unannealed tool steel.

TEMPERING

For most of the things we want, the final hardness of the steel has to come between the fully hardened and fully annealed states. By reducing some of the hardness, the tendency to brittleness is also reduced. The required hardness of a particular tool is found by tempering, which is done after hardening. The steel is heated to redness and quenched to harden it. It is again heated to a certain temperature, which varies according to the intended use, when it is quenched again.

If we had to measure the temperature, most of us with limited equipment would be in difficulty. Fortunately, there are colored oxides that form on a smooth bright surface of tool steel at definite temperatures. By watching the formation of these oxides and quenching at the right moment, you can get the correct temper without special equipment. The oxides will still be there after quenching; you can check results. Remember that the oxides are only a clue to temperature. You can get the same colors on mild steel, but that does not mean you have done anything to the hardness of the metal. When you are dealing with tool steel, it is only the part that was previously brought to redness in hardening that will be tempered. Nevertheless, you will see the oxide colors on other parts.

The oxide colors come in rainbow formation in a definite sequence. They can be seen on a clean, polished surface. Heating to harden takes away the polished effect. If you start with a bright surface, it can be rubbed bright again, after heating and quenching, by using emery cloth or a piece of sandstone.

To familiarize yourself with the colors, have a length of flat steel, perhaps 12 inches long, with one surface rubbed bright. Hold it by one end and heat near the middle with a flame. Once colors have started appearing there, withdraw the flame and only return it briefly, if necessary, until the whole set of colors is spreading from the heated part. If you keep the heat to the minimum necessary, each band of color will widen as it spreads so you get a better idea of the color sequence and the way the colors blend into each other. Overheating, or quick heating, will produce much narrower bands of color. The sequence of colors and their shades, with examples of tools tempered to them, is shown in Table 3-1.

Table 3-1. Tempering Colors.

Color of Oxide	Tools
Light yellow	Files
Yellow	—
Dark yellow	Chisels
Brown	Shears, scissors
Dark Brown	Knives, punches
Brown/purple	Axes
Light purple	Hoes, spades
Dark purple	Saws
Blue	Screwdrivers, springs

Annealing should be done before working on the steel; usually you make the tool completely before hardening and tempering it.

As a practical example of hardening and tempering, make a screwdriver from a piece of ¼-inch round tool steel. If it is newly annealed steel, file the taper at the end (Fig. 3-1A). If you prefer an awl, you could make a point. At the other end, file a square point for driving into a handle. Brighten the working end with abrasive. If you do not know if the steel has been annealed, your first attempts at filing will show you. If you cannot file, do not continue because that would ruin the tool. Anneal the steel before going further.

Heat the screwdriver end to redness for a distance of up to 1 inch and quench in water. Lower vertically into the water (Fig. 3-1B). If the tool goes in sideways, the slight unevenness of quenching might cause cracking. The end is now hardened and brittle; treat it gently. Brighten all of that end with emery cloth or other abrasive.

Use a blow-lamp flame to heat the rod a few inches back from the end (Fig. 3-1C). Watch the oxide colors form. They will spread outward. Those that go away from the working end are of no consequence. Keep the heating to a minimum once the colors form so that they spread in wide bands. When the blue color reaches the end, again quench the steel vertically in water. If you are satisfied that you have the right color at the end, clean off the colors and the whole tool with emery cloth, and fit a handle.

If you make a mistake and quench too late or too early, you must go back to hardening again before making another attempt at tempering. This method

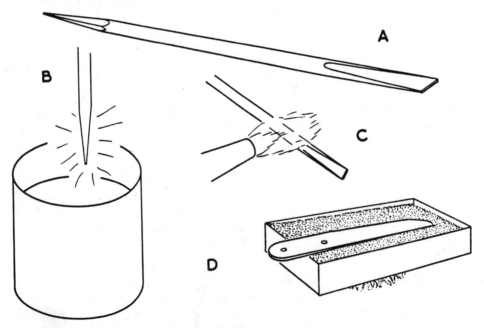

Fig. 3-1. A screwdriver end is hardened and tempered with a flame (A-C). A blade may be heated on sand (D).

works with any pointed tool or even one with a broad end, like a chisel. You can harden and temper a chisel for cutting rock or metal or deal with the end of a pick ax or other end-cutting tool.

If you work quickly, it is possible to harden and temper such a tool end with one heating. Heat the end to harden it, as just described, but when you quench the red hot end do not plunge the whole tool into water. Immerse enough to cool the red end and a little further, leaving plenty of heat still in the bar a few inches from the end. Quickly rub the end, and a few inches back, bright with abrasive and watch for the oxide colors coming along from the hot part. When you get the correct color on the end, immerse the whole tool endwise and it will be correctly tempered.

If you want to harden and temper a larger area—as would be necessary for the cutting edge of a knife, hoe, or other tool with a long or broad edge—you have to adopt a different method because local heating would give a patchy result. It might be possible to fan a blow-lamp flame over an area to get the degree of temper, but that is a chancy method.

For a piece of plate steel or other tool, such as a knife blade that is broad and not very thick, have it cleaned bright, and then heat it just to redness as evenly as possible all over the part that includes the cutting edge to harden it. Quench it quickly and clean it bright again.

Have a tray of sand ready. It should be a metal container rather larger than the metal to be heated for tempering and the sand should be about ½ inch thick. Put this over a flame to drive out moisture in the sand. Put the steel on the sand (Fig. 3-1D) and heat from below. The sand will spread the heat fairly evenly. At first you could immerse the steel in the sand to quicken its heating, but once the sand and steel get warm have the steel on top and watch as oxides form. Once they begin to appear, they will change quickly. Be prepared to act as soon as the color you want comes. Use pliers or tongs to lift the steel and drop it in the water. If you get it wrong, you must go back to hardening again before trying tempering a second time.

There is obviously a limit to the size of the tool that can be hardened and tempered by these methods, but many garden and farm cutting tools are within the practical range. If a tool part needs to be stronger than could be expected with mild steel, it is possible to use tool steel without hardening and tempering it and still find the results satisfactory. It is only when a cutting edge that will last has to be provided that hardening and tempering is essential. Tools that have to cut wood and metal are obvious examples, and tools to cut hay and other crops are other examples. For a tool such as a garden hoe that only has to cut soil, a reasonable life can be expected from an untreated blade. Moreover, its edge can be revived by filing.

NONFERROUS METALS

Most metals used in garden and yard tools are varieties of steel, but some others (described as nonferrous, because they lack iron) have their uses. The term *metal* is loosely applied to alloys as well as pure metals. None of the other common metals are as strong as steel, but most of them are easier to work and have better resistance to corrosion.

Copper is a soft, reddish metal that is now little used without being alloyed to other metals. Copper has been used for pipes because it suits their manufacture and copper pipes are easily bent. The only way that copper can become hard is by work hardening. If it is hammered, rolled, or other-wise worked, it could reach a stage where it gets hard; so much so that if nothing is done about it, it will crumble and crack. It can be annealed by heating to redness, and then by either cooling quickly or slowly. To a certain extent it will age harden if left as is, but in the annealed state it is very ductile.

Sheet copper can be hammered into quite deep bowl shapes, but it will have to be annealed many times in the process. If something made of sheet copper is to be brought to maximum hardness after the desired shape has been reached, it has to be *planished* (hammered all over), while supported on a stake or anvil, so the metal is squeezed at each blow between the hammer and the supporting steel surface.

Zinc is a metal that is seldom used alone today. It is a drab grey color and difficult to polish. At one time it was used for kitchen utensils because of its considerable resistance to corrosion and the ease with which it could be soldered. Perforated zinc sheets can still be obtained. They had much use in pioneer days for food storage cabinets, before the days of refrigeration, as they let cooling draughts through but kept flies out.

BRASS

Zinc is alloyed with copper to make brass. The quality and characteristics of the resulting alloy depend on the proportions of the two base metals. In any case the result is yellow: paler if the zinc proportion is high and more golden if there is more copper. Sheet brass is made with a fairly high copper content and it can be worked and annealed in the same way as copper (although it is never as soft or ductile). Brass takes a good polish to produce an attractive appearance. Brass parts on something mainly wood or another metal always gives a high-quality appearance.

Brass for machining contains more zinc. Rods can be machined cleanly, but this quality brass will break if an attempt is made to bend it. Where bending rather than machining is intended, rods and strips are made with copper and zinc proportions more like sheet material. Brass tubes will take slight bends, but they will also machine; pieces of brass tube make attractive ferrules on handles.

SPELTER

The melting point of an alloy is always lower than the melting points of its individual metals. This is taken advantage of in the making of *hard solder* or *spelter* for use in brazing joints using a flame. Copper and zinc in the correct proportions for a low melting point will form the spelter used in these joints. It is possible to vary the proportions so a spelter with a low melting point can be used near a joint made with a spelter having a higher melting point, and without the first joint separating. The melting point can be made even lower by adding silver. The resulting *silver* solder is obviously expensive and unlikely to be used on garden tools. However, there are low-melting-point hard solders obtainable with less expensive alloyed metals.

Brass and copper will corrode, but not to the same extent as iron and steel. Polishing gives a resistance to corrosion. When corrosion occurs, it is a greenish powder that rarely goes very deep. The initial corrosion provides a barrier to further corrosion. This can be seen in the green roofs of some old buildings where the copper sheathing has turned green, but will then last a very long time.

TIN AND LEAD

Tin can be alloyed with copper to make bronze; the sheet alloy is sometimes called *gilding metal*. Bronze has a better resistance to salt water corrosion than brass so it is used on boats. In an extreme case, saltwater will take the zinc out of brass so that screws and other parts crumble. Bronze has characteristics and appearance otherwise very similar to brass. The alloy could be used in similar situations on garden tools, if available, although it is not an alloy to choose specially.

Lead is a dull grey, heavy metal. Its concentrated weight governs most of its uses. If you want the most compact weight, it must be lead. Its melting point is low enough for it to be melted with an ordinary flame. Therefore it is possible to make a mold and pour in molten lead while using quite simple equipment.

Lead is obtainable as sheets that are very easily bent and formed. It has uses in gutters and as a valley between parts of a roof where it can be bent and cut to shape in position. Water pipes were once made of lead, but it is now known to be unsafe for carrying drinking water. In making tools, lead is more likely to be used to provide weight. There is no way of hardening or softening lead, but it has almost complete resistance to corrosion.

SOLDER

Lead and tin are alloyed together to make common or "tinman's" solder. The melting point is such that the solder can be made to flow with a soldering iron (actually a copper bit) or a flame. The proportions of the two metals affect the melting point and characteristics of the solder. At one time, a solder with a high lead content was used to make joints in lead pipes by *wiping*. This solder remained ductile enough before fully cooling for it to be wiped to shape with a suitable cloth or moleskin.

When most pots and pans were made of tinplate, soldering played a big part in construction and repairs. A tinsmith or tinman was a busy craftsman, while the travelling tinker made his living from repairs.

In making garden and yard tools and equipment, soldered tinplate can be the best way to make special containers, measures, planters, and similar things. For a one-off item, soldered tinplate can provide better and easier results than fabricating from other materials.

ALUMINUM

Aluminum is well known as a lightweight, silvery metal with a good resistance to corrosion but not much strength. Pure aluminum is very soft. Most material loosely described as aluminum has other metals alloyed, in very small quantities, for hardening and strengthening. Most aluminum tubes are of this type.

Sheet aluminum might be used for making special containers and similar things, but it cannot be soldered by normal methods. Therefore, joints have to be screwed, riveted, or joined in some mechanical way or by specialized welding.

Corrosion of aluminum is usually slight and it takes the form of a fine powder that can be brushed off. Many structures of aluminum used outdoors are left untreated. Iron and most other metals require paint or other protection from the weather. There is no way to anneal or harden aluminum to any appreciable extent.

RIVETS

Rivets are used to make more permanent joints in metal than screws or bolts and nuts. They can provide all the strength needed in themselves, but in many garden tools one or more rivets are used to keep the parts in the correct relation to each other while they are brazed or welded. In that case, the rivet is not expected to provide much strength in the finished tool. Therefore, it can be thinner. Because most parts being joined are steel, the rivets should normally be iron or steel. For purely locating purposes, copper rivets are easy to work. Aluminum is not compatible with brazing. If the rivets have to provide strength without the assistance of brazing or welding, they should be iron or steel.

In most small tools, the rivets can be ⅛ inch, ³⁄₁₆ inch, or ¼ inch diameter. They can be made from rod or you can buy rivets with prepared heads on one end. The common head is round (Fig. 3-2A) and sometimes called a *snap rivet*. It can be countersunk (Fig. 3-2B) and there are several other methods. Heads can be shaped in position with a ball-pane hammer (Fig. 3-2C), although a crosspane (Fig. 3-2D) has uses in getting a head edge close to the surface.

A tool called a *snap* or *set* has a hollow to match a particular rivet head and might have a hole to match the diameter of the rivet (Fig. 3-2E). The hole is used over the end of the rivet to set down tightly the metal parts the rivet end projects through (Fig. 3-2F). The hollow can be used to support a prepared head, with the tool held in a vise, while the other head is formed. If you hammer a round head to a reasonable shape, the snap can be used over it to finish its surface. Without the support of a snap, a prepared head resting on an iron block will flatten, but that might not matter. Without a snap, you can support a prepared head on a lead block to avoid damage to it.

A hole for a rivet should be a close fit to avoid bending the shank when the end is hammered. If you want the head to finish level, countersink the hole properly to make a head that will have sufficient strength. Estimate the amount of rivet end left standing to be enough to fill the countersink (Fig. 3-2H).

If you have to make a rivet from rod, cut it to sufficient length to make two heads. Support one end on an iron block or with a snap and start forming one

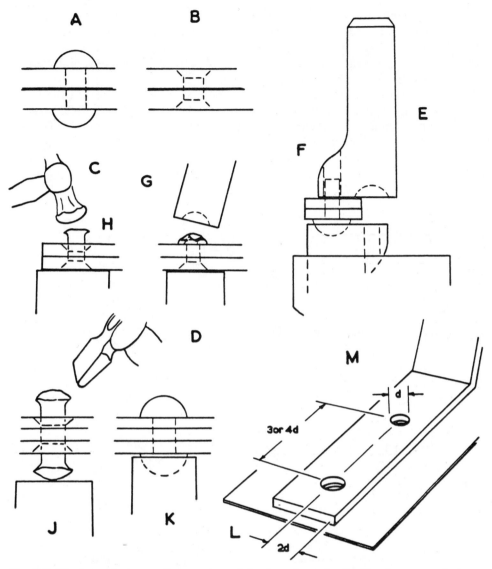

Fig. 3-2. Rivets can have round or countersunk heads and are closed with a hammer and set.

side. After a short time, work on the other side (Fig. 3-2J), and do this progressively until you have two good heads (Fig. 3-2K).

Rivet centers should be at least two diameters from an edge (Fig. 3-2L) and usually three or four diameters apart (Fig. 3-2M).

OTHER METAL FASTENERS

If you want to take a joint apart, as when making a tool with alternative heads, the parts can be held with nuts and bolts. If you need a "bolt" with a screw thread almost to its head, ask for a machine screw (Fig. 3-3A). If you ask for a "bolt," it will only be threaded a short distance from its end (Fig. 3-3B). If there is no good reason for using any other screwed connection, choose hexagonal nuts and bolt heads that are made with precision and suit standard wrenches. Normally, put washers under bolt heads and nuts (Fig. 3-3C).

If one or more parts have to rotate on a bolt, you need to prevent the nut from loosening. The traditional way is to add a plain locknut (Fig. 3-3D), and then with two wrences the lower nut is tightened against the upper one. There are many nuts available with friction of some sort built in (Fig. 3-3E). They hold without further assistance. A castellated nut (Fig. 3-3F), with the bolt end drilled for a cotter pin, is more often used in machinery and is less likely to be needed

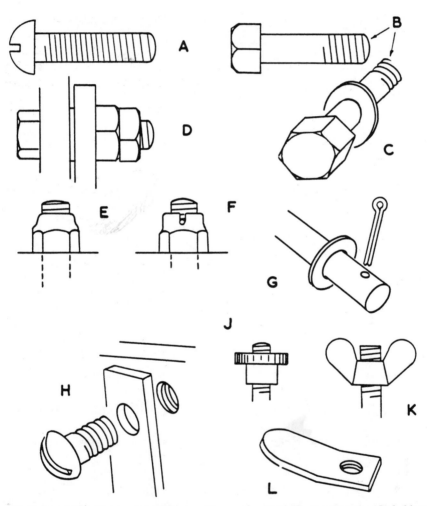

Fig. 3-3. Screws and bolts are used with several types of nuts (A-F). A cotter pin (G) holds parts on a rod. A thread in a part can take the place of a nut (H). Some nuts can be turned without a wrench (J-L).

in garden equipment. However, a cotter pin and washer (Fig. 3-3G) is a good way of retaining a loose part on a rod.

If one part is thick enough and you have the necessary screwing equipment, you can dispense with a nut by driving a bolt end into a threaded hole (Fig. 3-3H).

A nut tightened with a wrench is most secure, if you want to be able to change a part or make an adjustment, but you have to find the wrench. To avoid that, you can use a hand-operated nut. For a small part it can be knurled (Fig. 3-3J). For more leverage it is better to use a wing or butterfly nut (Fig. 3-3K). In some situations, it might be better to cut a thread through a hole at the end of a flat strip (Fig. 3-3L) to give you more of a wrench action.

CONICAL DEVELOPMENTS

Some long-handled tools are attached to the wood handles with tapered tubular parts, usually secured with one or two screws through holes. The conical part can be cut square across (Fig. 3-4A) or it looks neat if shaped to a central screw hole (Fig. 3-4B). The lower side can be open. Therefore, it is possible to get a reasonable shape for the sheet steel before bending by doing little special marking out.

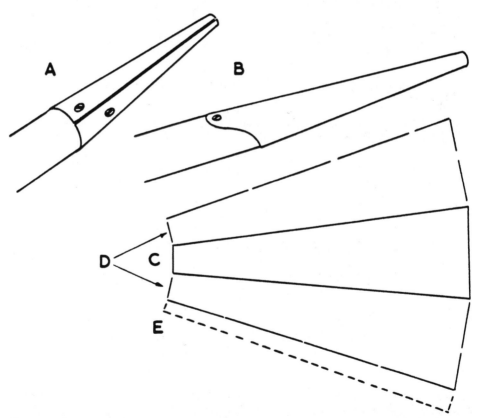

Fig. 3-4. Sheet metal for a tapered socket can have its developed shape set out approximately.

For a simple truncated cone, you can draw the size you want the finished part to be (Fig. 3-4C) and mark each side of it the same (Fig. 3-4D) using a card template. That gives you a width of three times the diameter. For a full-width closed cone, it should be three and one-seventh (the relation between diameter and circumference of a circle) times the diameter. The odd fraction can be left as the gap at the bottom or you can add a little when you cut out (Fig. 3-4E).

Round the ends and you have a shape that can be rolled to the final cone (as nearly accurate as it needs to be on most tools). If the top is to be shaped, you can draw in the outline freehand on half of the development, and then reverse it on the other side.

For a more exact truncated cone, particularly if the large end is to be curved, the shape should be set out geometrically. Draw a side view (Fig. 3-5A). If you want a shaped top, continue to where the point would be if cut square (Fig. 3-5B). At the small end, extend the lines until they meet (Fig. 3-5C). With that point as center, draw curves that will be the ends of the developed shaped. Draw a line for one edge to the center (Fig. 3-5D) and measure three and one-seventh

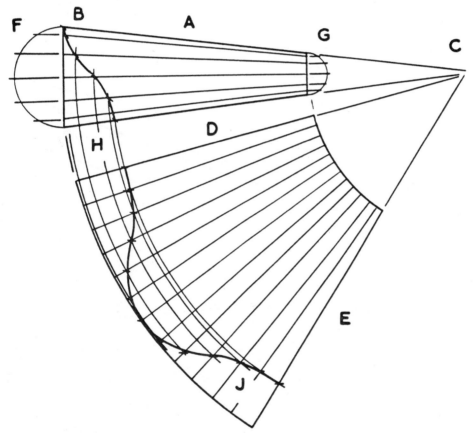

Fig. 3-5. A more accurate development of a tapered socket has ordinates transferred from a side view to the open shape.

times the diameter around the outer curve for a line to mark the other side of the development (Fig. 3-5E). That gives you the shape to cut the metal to roll into a square ended conical object, if that is what you need.

If there is to be a curved end or there is any other shaping to be done, you have to draw lines (ordinates) on the side view and repeat them in appropriate places on the development. You can then mark points on the curve and join them. Draw semicircles on the ends (Figs. 3-5F and G) and divide them into equal divisions; six should do (making 12 in a full circle). Project the points to the ends and join them. Divide the outer curve of the development into 12 and draw lines toward the center. Working around the center, project crossings on the side view lines to the matching lines on the development (Fig. 3-5H). Draw through these points to get the developed shape of the end curve (Fig. 3-5J).

4
CHAPTER

Rustic Construction

The use of natural poles and logs is particularly appropriate to the construction of things for use outdoors in the yard and garden. The wood in its more natural form will often look better in these surroundings than boards and posts that have been sawn square and possibly planed as well. Obviously, there are situations where the prepared wood is more appropriate, but if you have a supply of wood from felling or trimming you might consider using it for several projects outdoors. If the wood is unsuitable for sawing into boards, using it "as it is" gives it a new life.

Wood obtained by clearing land will be full of sap that will soon dry out. Such wood will shrink and might split. In particular, cracks are liable to pass through nail holes and weaken fastenings, even to the extent of joints collapsing. If you must use "green" wood, keep it for the cruder structures such as rough fencing. For better construction, the wood should be allowed to season in ventilated but dry space for some time (preferably a couple of years).

What you do about bark depends on the wood. With some woods, the bark is very firmly attached to the wood whether it is newly felled or has had time to season. In that case, the bark could be left on and you might find this improves appearances in a garden situation. If the bark is easy to peel with a hatchet or chisel, it should be removed before the wood is used. With many woods, the bark will peel unaided after the wood underneath has dried. If you use such wood with the bark on, next year you might find the structure you have built has become a patchwork of partly peeled wood that looks unattractive. In general, if bark will peel without too much effort, it is better to remove it before using the wood.

A section of log more than a few inches thick will take a very long time to season if left as it is. It is better to plan what you will do with it, and then cut the wood to approximate size. You could saw it across to a little more than the final length. If something is to be made with half or less of the diameter, split the wood lengthwise. Seasoning times are related to thickness rather than length. The more you can reduce the cross-section the better. It is very probable that cracks will develop at the ends of pieces as they dry. If the wood is longer than necessary before seasoning, you can cut off any ends that split later.

If you have the skill, you might split a log centrally with one heavy blow with an ax. For most workers it is safer and more accurate to use wedges. Ideally, the wedge should be steel. It is, however, possible to start a split with a hatchet, and then drive in a wooden wedge (Fig. 4-1A). As the split develops, another wedge can be driven into the side (Fig. 4-1B) to continue the split. Then the first wedge can be removed and entered again further along the split (Fig. 4-1C) and so on, in turn, if it is a long log.

The traditional tool for cleaving thinner wood is a froe (Fig. 4-1D). If a froe is unavailable, something like it can be improvised with a strip of flat stiff steel. In use, it is first driven into the end of the wood like a wedge. By rocking the handle (Fig. 4-1E), the split can be levered open and extended along the wood. This is particularly successful with recently felled wood.

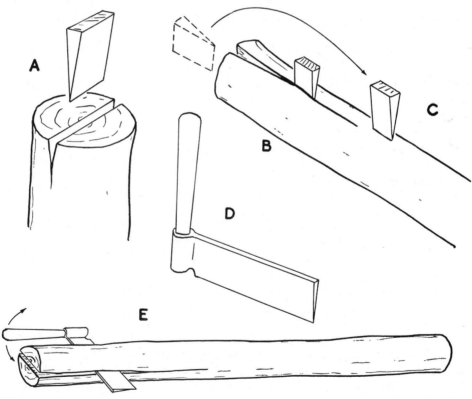

Fig. 4-1. Wood can be split with a wedge (A-C). The traditional tool is a froe (D,E).

JOINTS

Much rustic construction is simple hammer and nail work that will suffice in many situations. In better assemblies, the nails can be supplemented with cut joints. These will not have the precision of many joints in sawn and planed wood, but they serve to increase strength where it is required. Unprotected steel nails will soon be attacked by moisture in the wood, as well as any in the atmosphere, so use nails protected by galvanizing or another process.

There is a great temptation in rustic work to hammer in nails without preparation, but it is wise to assume that the wood you are using will shrink eventually, and that could mean splits at nail holes. To reduce this risk, drill clearance holes in the top pieces, and for all but the finer nails, pilot holes in the lower pieces. This is particularly important near ends. Clenching is often advisable if you can take a nail through and turn over its point while the head is supported with another hammer or an iron block.

Cleft wood can be joined with the flat faces together. So far as possible, in this and other nailed joints, drive two nails so they do not come in the same grain lines either way. This usually means arranging them diagonally across a joint (Fig. 4-2A). If the two parts are similar sections, the nails can be driven from opposite sides (Fig. 4-2B). If sections are different, it is stronger to nail through the thinner into the thicker.

Round poles can often be nailed directly to each other, but it is better to prepare flat meeting surfaces with either a hatchet or a saw and chisel (Fig. 4-2C). You could shave toward an end of or chop out a hollow further along a pole. In any case, do not weaken the wood by cutting too deeply.

Two crossing poles can each be cut like a halving joint (Fig. 4-2D). In rustic construction, it is unusual for poles to be crossed at the same level. Usually only a small amount is cut out of each piece. Saw across the grain at the limits of the cuts and chop out the waste with a chisel. Another way of dealing with a crossing (which is appropriate when you are uncertain, until you assemble, where the crossing will come on one piece) is to leave a part round, but hollow the other to take it (Fig. 4-2E).

If pieces meet like a letter T, sometimes one can go over the other and be nailed. If they are to meet in the same plane, a simple nail through will not be very effective or strong. It is better to cut a notch for the end to go in (Fig. 4-2F). That would be even stronger if the end is shaved to make a parallel joint (Fig. 4-2G). Another joint that can be cut entirely with a saw has a V-shaped socket and an end to match it (Fig. 4-2H). Nails go through the long part into the end part in all these joints.

The V-cut is also suitable if the joint is diagonal (Fig. 4-2J). The squared end of the round piece then merely fits in, but the circumferences of the two pieces do not make a very close match. A better appearance is obtained by altering the shape of the notch and cutting the end to fit (Fig. 4-2K). These joints are often nailed into the end grain, but you get a better grip if the nail goes diagonally across the grain (Fig. 4-2L).

Another method of construction is very similar to doweling. The end of one

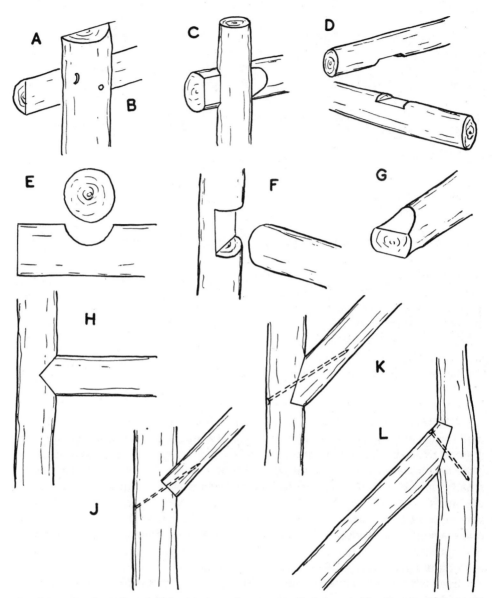

Fig. 4-2. Natural wood can be joined in several ways; usually it is a combination of notching and nailing.

piece is tapered to a smaller round and driven into a hole drilled in the other piece. A drawknife or chisel will do the tapering. The hole can be made with a large bit in an electric drill, slightly more laboriously with a bit in a brace, or with an auger. In the simplest form of the joint, a hole is drilled about halfway through one piece, and then the tapered end becomes a drive fit in it (Fig. 4-3A). If the wood is dry, you can use a waterproof glue in the joint. Most glues are ineffective if the wood contains much sap. A nail could be driven across the joint.

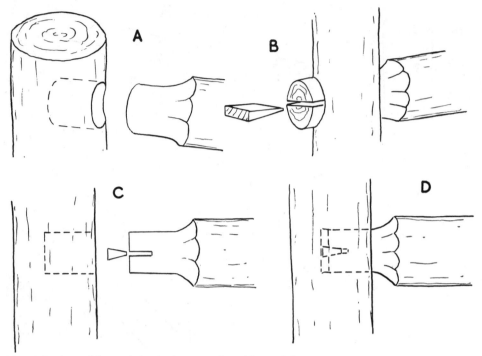

Fig. 4-3. An end into a hole can be strengthened by wedging.

A similar joint can have the hole drilled right through and the round end made long enough to pass through and project a little. Care is needed in tapering the end to leave a sufficient amount parallel, and in order to make a reasonably close fit within the hole. It might be sufficient to leave the joint as a drive fit or a nail can be driven across. A better way of securing is to put a saw cut in the end and drive in a wedge (Fig. 4-3B). This should be arranged across so that the spreading force is resisted by end grain in the holed piece. The other way could cause a split. It is advisable to make the wedge of hardwood even if the parts being joined are softwood. You can saw off the surplus end when the wedge is as tight as you can get it.

Even when it is not appropriate for the hole to go right through, it is possible to tighten an end by what is called *fox wedging* in the "blind" hole. This is sometimes done in cabinetwork. Drill the hole at least halfway through and make the end to fit it. Put a saw cut across the end and make a short hardwood wedge to fit it. It is common to give this a more obtuse angle than one for use outside. Put the wedge in the saw cut, arranged across the grain of the other piece (Fig. 4-3C), and then drive the parts together so the wedge pushing on the bottom of the hole spreads the end of the dowel (Fig. 4-3D).

There are not many uses for screws in rustic work, but you can use nuts and bolts (preferably galvanized). Screws do not hold very well in wood that is not fully seasoned, and neither do the square necks of coach bolts. It is better to use bolts with heads to take a wrench, and put washers under them to spread the pressure. This is particularly important if it is wood with the bark still on. With a wrench on the bolt head and another on the nut, you can make a really tight joint.

DESIGN

Much rustic work is comparatively crude. That will not matter for many things and is acceptable, but it is important to design properly. It is possible to build what seems satisfactory at first, and then find the assembly becomes shaky or goes out of shape. All of this can be avoided if you remember the value of the

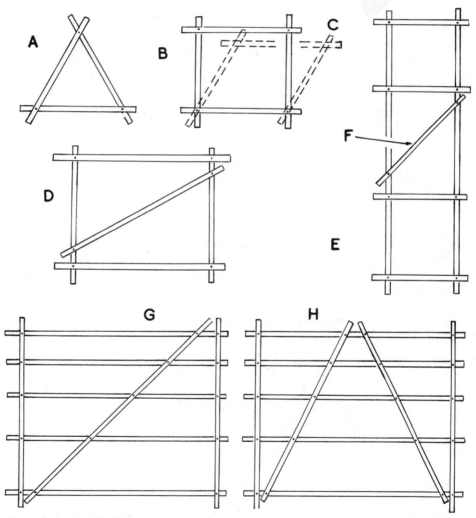

Fig. 4-4. A triangle (A) cannot be pushed out of shape like a four-sided figure (B,C). Diagonals are used to triangulate structures (D-H).

triangle. You cannot push a triangle out of shape. That is probably the most important design consideration when fashioning a structure from poles.

If you join three poles with one nail at each joint (Fig. 4-4A), it retains it shape. Do the same with four poles (Fig. 4-4B) and you can push it over (Fig. 4-4C). If you add a diagonal, that makes it into two triangles (Fig. 4-4D) and you cannot alter the shape. Every square does not have to be given a diagonal. Suppose you are making a tall, narrow frame for roses to climb (Fig. 4-4E). A diagonal in one panel will stiffen the whole thing (Fig. 4-4F).

Suppose there are several horizontal poles on two uprights. Without diagonal bracing they could go out of shape. One diagonal across the lot provides triangulation (Fig. 4-4G) or a pair meeting at the center would serve the same purpose (Fig. 4-4H). Sometimes diagonals are taken both ways so that they cross. That will add a little more stiffness, but it is done mainly for the sake of appearance.

In some assemblies it is better to keep the diagonals out of the way by making them struts at one or more corners of a four-sided assembly. This is almost as effective as full diagonals. Of course, driving uprights into the ground can provide all the stiffness in a frame that is otherwise four-sided without diagonals. Even then the stiffness might be imagined as coming from a diagonal from the point in the ground to the surface.

THREE-LEGGED STOOL

The strength of a triangle can be taken a step further in noting that three legs will stand without wobbling on any surface. Our ancestors knew this and took care of unevenness in floors by making chairs, stools, and tables with three legs instead of the more obvious four. The milkmaid's stool for sitting anywhere in a cow shed is an obvious example, but three-legged seats can still have useful applications in a modern yard or garden. The average lawn might seem level until you find your usual seat will not stand without rocking. If you want to sit on an undeveloped surface, the usual folding chairs will not settle. Have a seat with three legs and it will be stable anywhere.

A version of the milking stool can have a round top (Fig. 4-5A) or you can use a split piece of log to make a rectangular seat (Fig. 4-5B). The round top could be a disc cut across a log, but some sections tend to dry out with radical cracks. Make sure your crosscut disc is dry and sound before using it. The alternative is to cut a disc with the grain across.

1. For the round stool, the disc can be about 12 inches diameter and 2 inches thick. To get the three legs equally spaced, draw a circle about 8 inches diameter—either on the disc or on paper—and step off the radius around it. The holes will come on alternate marks (Fig. 4-5C).

2. Prepare the pieces for the legs (perhaps 1½ inches in diameter and 15 inches long). The holes and the tapered ends can be about 1 inch in diameter.

3. The holes to be drilled at angles that will put the bottoms of the legs outside the rim of the top (Fig. 4-5D). This is advisable for stability.

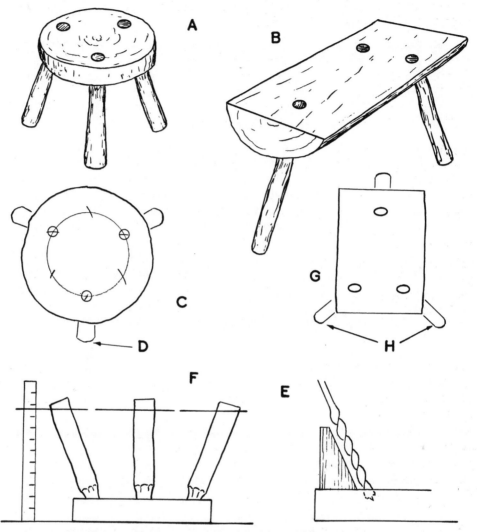

Fig. 4-5. *Using three legs allows a stool to stand without wobbling on any surface.*

4. If the holes can be made on a drill press, the wood can be packed up so the angles are drilled the same. If they are drilled freehand, a block of wood can be used as a guide to the angle. (Fig. 4-5E).

5. Taper the legs to drive into the top, preferably to extend and be wedged, and then trim them level.

6. Invert the stool on a flat surface, measure equal heights for the legs (Fig. 4-5F), and cut them off. Remove raggedness and round the bottoms so there is no risk of a sharp stone breaking out the grain.

7. A stool with a split log top can be made in a very similar way. Arrange the leg holes so there is one central and two as widely spaced as the wood will allow (Fig. 4-5G).

8. Drill the holes at angles that will allow the legs to come outside the outline of the top (Fig. 4-5H).

9. Make and fit the legs in the same way as for the round stool. Level their bottoms after inverting and measuring, as before.

10. In both cases, level the tops by planing and sanding, but leave other parts as they are, to preserve the rustic effect.

FOUR-LEGGED BENCH SEAT

If a split log is to be used for a seat longer than needed for just one person, it is advisable to give it four legs. A long, three-legged seat could become unstable if the first person sits at the one-leg end. A bench seat suitable for two or three people, made from half a log possibly 12 inches in diameter, will be fairly heavy. Therefore, it is likely to be located in one position and rarely moved. The four legs can be bedded down level so the seat will not wobble. The legs could also be thicker than in the lighter seats described earlier. For a bench 6 feet long and about 12 inches wide, the legs should be about 3 inches thick (Fig. 4-6A).

1. The split log may need its top leveled if the split followed wavy grain. It need not be exactly half a log, if you want to make it lighter, providing there is sufficient width if the split is off-center. Of course, splitting one log gives you pieces suitable for two bench seats, unless you have other uses for the second piece.

2. A long split log might leave edges that could be thin enough to be weak or sharp enough to be uncomfortable. This is particularly so if branches or other projections occur where the split comes. In that case, either remove just where these parts are (Fig. 4-6B) or make a straight cut along square to the top surface (Fig. 4-6C).

3. If the log section is fairly thick, there is no need to take the legs right through. If the legs are 3 inches thick, the holes should not be less than 1½ inches in diameter. If the bench is to be located in one position, it is advisable to let the legs into the ground. In that case, they could be almost upright (Fig. 4-6D). If they are actually vertical, you could not put a pair very far apart because there would not be sufficient thickness of log to drill nearer the edges.

4. If the legs are not to go into the ground, they should spread to come outside the width of the seat top and be near the end (Fig. 4-6E). Use an angled block of wood as a guide, but as you are drilling on the curved surface you will have to work mostly by eye. Slight variations between legs will not matter.

5. Take the holes in to a depth between 1½ and 2 times their diameter (Fig. 4-6F). Anything less might become loose or let the legs wobble.

6. Prepare the legs to make a close fit. It might be sufficient to just drive them in, but fox wedging will strengthen the joints (Fig. 4-6G).

Materials List for Four-legged Bench Seat		
1 half log	72 ×	12
4 legs	18 ×	3

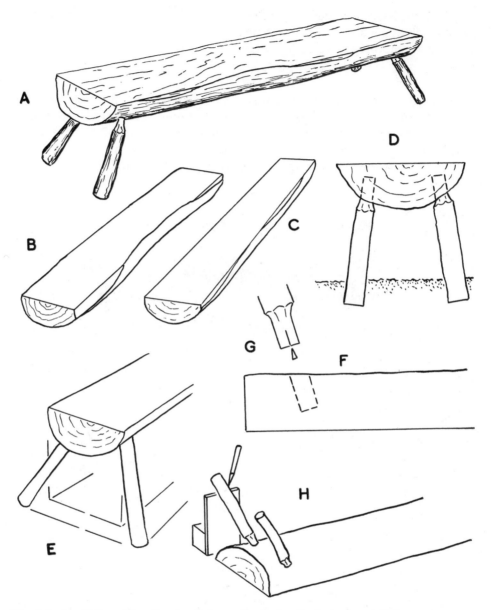

Fig. 4-6. *A split log will make a bench top, and splaying the legs gives stability.*

7. If the legs are to be let into the ground, it would be unwise to point them because that might cause them to penetrate more than you want when the seat is in use. It is better to leave them cut square and sink them in sunk holes (rather than try to drive them in). In very soft soil, a flat piece of wood could be buried under each leg.

8. If the legs are to stand on the surface, turn the bench over and measure from its top to get all the legs the same length. You can do this by measuring, or using a temporary gauge. (Fig. 4-6H).

LOG TROUGH

A hollowed log trough in which plants can be grown makes a simple variation on the bench seat. Similar legs can be fitted, but they need only be short if all you want to do is steady the log just above the ground (Fig. 4-7A). Size can be whatever you prefer, but there must be enough wood to make a hollow 6 inches or more deep (unless all you want to grow are small surface flowers).

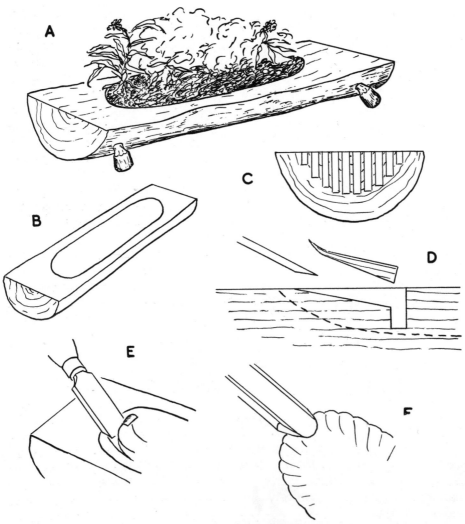

Fig. 4-7. A log can be hollowed by progressive drilling and chopping out with a gouge or chisel.

1. Construction details are the same as the bench seat. It is advisable to complete the fitting of legs before doing any hollowing because the legs will provide stability for the wood while you remove the waste.

2. Decide on the outline of the hollow on the surface. Do not go too close to the sides and keep further in from the ends. The cut short grain might eventually open in splits if you do not leave much solid wood there. You could use a long ellipse, but it will probably be best to keep parallel to the sides and round the ends (Fig. 4-7B).

3. Fortunately, you do not have to produce a smooth inside to the hollow as it will be hidden by soil, but you must aim to get a reasonable shape even if you do not achieve it exactly. Bear in mind the shape you want, but remember to allow for any variations on the outside of the log and do not take the wood too thin. Much depends on the wood. With softwoods you should leave more thickness than you would with hardwoods. Allow for the legs going into more solid wood past the beginning of the hollow at each end or only just where it starts.

4. At the center of the hollow, make a series of holes approximating to the cross section of the shape you want (Fig. 4-7C). These holes do two things: they give you a shape to work to, and they prevent splits developing as you chop out wood towards the center.

5. It will help to drill more holes. You can do this with an electric drill or you can use a plunge router (if the router will take a bit large enough to be worthwhile). The holes are to break up the waste wood that has to be removed—so you can chop to a hole and break out the chip—without having to cut a long way each time (Fig. 4-7D).

6. You can remove a lot of waste with a wide stiff chisel, used with its bevel downward (Fig. 4-7E). If you use it the other way it will try to go deeper, but with the bevel down, you can alter the angle of cut and follow the curved bottom. Do all chopping from the ends toward the center.

7. A better tool is a large, stiff gouge that is beveled on the outside. Toward completion, this will make a better shape than a chisel (Fig. 4-7F).

8. If you have to complete with chisels, a narrow one will follow the wide one to make a reasonable finish. It is only the visable part around the edge of the hollow that matters in any case (providing you have scooped out enough for the soil).

SLAB-LEGGED BENCH SEAT

When a log is cut into boards at a sawmill, the outside has to be taken off to leave the remainder either with two parallel sides or with four flat sides making a rectangular section with rounded corners. If the log is irregular in length, the pieces cut off the sides might be thin in places and quite thick elsewhere. The slabs off the sides can be used for bench tops (although they are not half logs), and particularly if they came off logs of very large section and are plenty wide enough in themselves. If you use one of these slab offcuts, make sure there is at least 3 inches or 4 inches thickness to provide stiffness and adequate wood to take legs. There could be round legs, but in this case a pair of slab legs are suggested (Fig. 4-8).

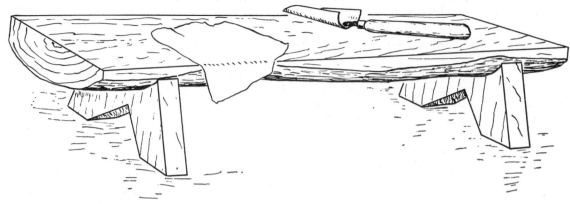

Fig. 4-8. A split log can be made into a bench with a pair of substantial slab legs.

1. These slabs will have finer edges than half logs and the edges might wander more than can be accepted. In that case, you could make straight, parallel cuts square to the surface (Fig. 4-9A) in order to fully remove all waviness or to just take off the greater curves.

2. The legs are pieces with parallel thickness. In converting logs to boards, a sawmill will have to discard parts of boards cut after removing the rounded outer slabs. These slabs can be cut for legs. If not, you must use boards 2 inches or more thick for legs under most tops (whether one-man seats or longer benches).

3. Stand the legs upright near the ends of the top or splayed out slightly toward the ends. There is less need to get a wide splay as for individual round legs. Mark where the legs are to come and their thickness on the wood (Fig. 4-9B).

4. Cut the slots for the legs with a chain saw. If you do not trust yourself to work accurately with a chain saw, use a handsaw, and then chop out the waste with chisel (Fig. 4-9C). Try to get the slots fairly deep. This depends on how thick the wood is, but a good depth is needed if the legs are to be a drive fit.

5. Have the grain upright in the legs. They could just have upright sides, but if there is enough width to cut they are better tapered (Fig. 4-9D). So that they are better able to stand on any surface without wobbling, cut away the bottoms with a V (Fig. 4-9E) or a curve (Fig. 4-9F).

6. Ideally, the legs will make a drive fit and will need no other fastening. Use a piece of scrap wood to spread the load as you drive them in (Fig. 4-9G).

7. If a leg is too thick, it can be pared thinner carefully. If it is too thin, shavings or thin pieces of wood can be used beside it in its slot. With the risk of expansion and contraction in use, it is advisable to provide more fastening, even when the joints are tight at first assembly. Nails can be driven down through the top (Fig. 4-9H), but they would be more effective diagonal underneath (Fig. 4-9J).

8. If the wood is dry enough to take glue, you can glue the legs into their slots; then, drill down through the top for several dowels glued into each leg (Fig. 4-9K). There is no satisfactory way of wedging legs and screws would not be very successful.

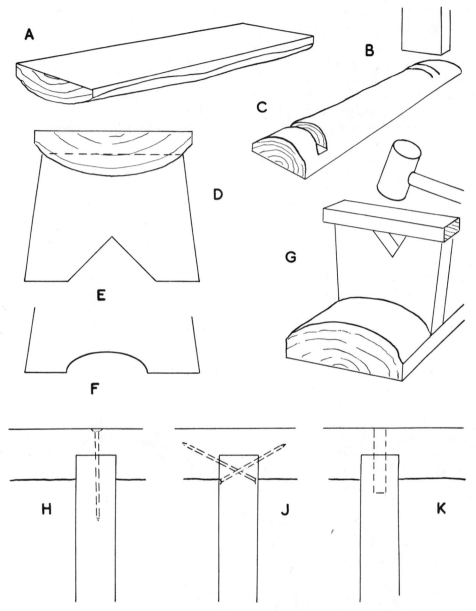

Fig. 4-9. Slots for the legs must match. They can be secured by nails or dowels.

LOG SEAT WITH BACK

Any stool or bench without a back can only provide limited comfort. If anyone wants to sit for long, a backrest is needed. There are ways of fitting backs to log seats, but most of them involve prepared wood and are described later. It is possible to make a simple, one-man half-log seat into a chair with a back that still keeps the rustic appearance and will fit in with a wild garden background

(Fig. 4-10). There may not be the comfort of a shaped or upholstered chair, but it is a step on from a simple flat seat.

1. Make a seat from half a log, with three legs, as already described. Allow for 12 inches to 15 inches at the two-leg end forward of where the back will come. The single leg hole must come far enough behind the back for the short grain not to be a source of weakness. That means a flat top 12 inches to 15 inches wide and probably 20 inches or more long. Round the front corners.

2. Prepare the seat parts, but do not fit the legs until after the back has been fitted.

Fig. 4-10. A three-leg stool is made more comfortable by the addition of a back.

3. The back is split from a log. It need not be as wide as the seat. Have it longer than needed until after making the joint.

4. Thin the bottom of the back to about 1½ inches (Fig. 4-11B) and on that, mark the width of tenon (Fig. 4-11B). The sides should be parallel, but it does not matter if there is a slight taper in thickness.

5. Mark the mortise in the seat. The back should fit about 15 degrees to upright (Fig. 4-11C). Cut through the forward edge of the mortise to that angle,

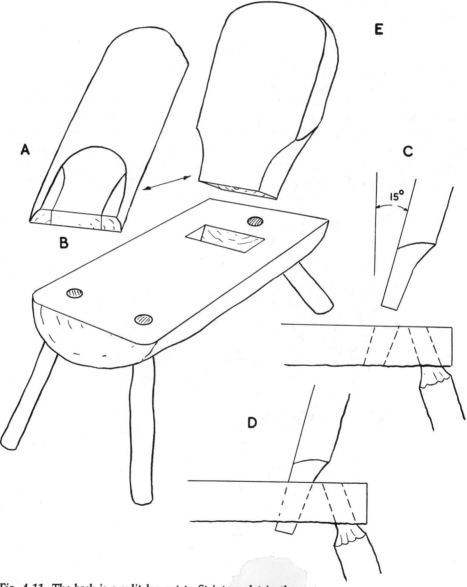

Fig. 4-11. The back is a split log cut to fit into a slot in the seat.

with enough waste to allow for working with the drill and chisel, but leave some waste wood at the rear edge of the mortise to trim later.

6. Cut the rear edge of the mortise progressively so you can try in the tenon. Get as close a fit as you can, but if it is not perfect the back will drive in and take care of slight inaccuracies. The tenon should go through and project slightly (Fig. 4-11D).

7. Round the top edge of the back to a curve you like the look of (Fig. 4-11E). The rounded back can be thinned toward the top if the full curve looks too bulky.

8. It should be sufficient to drive the back in. If it ever loosens, it can be driven further.

POLE CHAIR

If you have a supply of poles available, they could be made into a rustic chair. It will not have the comfort of one with upholstery or slung canvas or even a seat made from flat planed boards, but it is a piece of furniture that can be left outside and you can always put cushions in it for long use. The chair shown in Fig. 4-12 is intended to be made from poles all between 2 inches and 3 inches diameter. Their bark should have been peeled and they should be at least partially seasoned. Hardwood will be stronger and have a longer life, but a chair made from the more readily available fir and larch poles will have a reasonably long life. This is particularly true if it is soaked in preservative.

Fig. 4-12. This arm chair is made entirely from light poles.

Sizes will have to be adjusted to suit available materials. Those shown (Fig. 4-13) will give a reasonably roomy chair. It helps if you can find a pair of curved poles to make the back legs. If you have to use straight ones, slope them back slightly, and you can give the central support pieces a more comfortable angle by putting the crosspiece at the bottom in front of the legs and the top one at the back. If the legs have enough curve to provide a comfortable angle, both crosspieces are better at the back. The suggested construction uses bolts through for all parts that take much load. The fronts of the arms have dowel joints and the pieces making the back and seat could be nailed. Bolts about ⅜ of an inch diameter should be satisfactory.

The sequence of construction has the two sides made first as a pair. Choose poles that will give a reasonable match. Otherwise you might finish with a chair that is not level or has a twist in it. The poles that are fitted closely to form the seat and back could be slightly thinner. If you are cutting long poles, the bottoms can be used for the structure and the tops kept for seat and back. It helps to sort

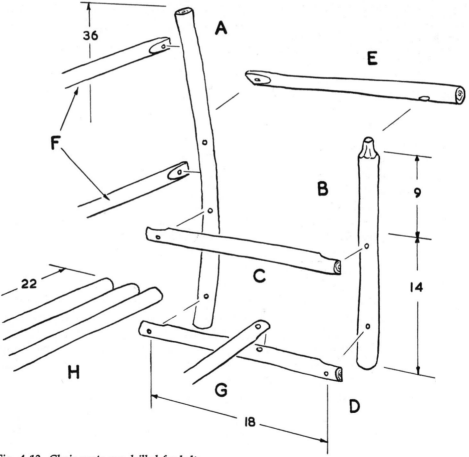

Fig. 4-13. Chair parts are drilled for bolts.

your sections of poles before starting construction in order to make sure you are using the most appropriate pieces for particular parts and to check that you have enough. It would be possible to use flat boards for the seat and back.

1. Select the pieces for the rear uprights (Fig. 4-13A). See that they will make a pair and mark the positions of the bolts.

2. Make the front uprights (Fig. 4-13B). Mark bolt positions from those on the rear legs. The seat level could be up to 2 inches higher at the front. You could make it level, but it would be wrong to risk the chair finishing with the seat front lower than the back.

3. Prepare the tops of the front uprights to dowel into the arms. These are the only doweled joints shown, but you can use them for the lower rails if you prefer.

4. Make the seat rails (Fig. 4-13C) and the lower rails (Fig. 4-13D). All four should be the same (with flattened ends where they bolt against the uprights). Do not thin them too much. If a pole is 2½ inches diameter, a flat about 1½ inches wide would be enough.

5. Drill the bolt holes for the rails and assemble the pair of sides with the rails attached. Make the arms. Drill them for the front dowels, and then swing each arm to the rear upright so as to mark the part to be flattened and drilled (Fig. 4-13E). The dowels may finish as drive fits or be fox wedged. Round the forward ends of the arms.

6. Make the rails that go across the back (Fig. 4-13F) and the bottom rail (Fig. 4-13G). If you do not consider a single rail across the bottom to be stiff enough, there could be two. The poles forming the seat will supplement the strength of this.

7. Bolt on the back and bottom rails. Have the chair standing on a level surface and check that it stands upright when viewed from any direction. Tighten all bolts fully.

8. Use these poles as necessary to fill the space. If sizes vary, have the thicker at the front. If poles taper slightly, they can be put on in alternate directions. If the poles are reasonably parallel, they can be fitted as they are (Fig. 4-13H). If there are inequalities or lumps where twigs were attached, it may be better to get meeting surfaces reasonably match by working with a chisel or plane.

9. Let the seat poles project through to come about level with the uprights. Nail them on. It would be wise to support under the seat rails while hammering to minimize shock and reduce the risk of splitting. In any case, drill clearance holes in the seat pieces and pilot holes, and if necessary, in the rails.

10. The back is made up of vertical poles arranged similarly to those of the seat. They could be the thinnest pieces in your collection of poles. Tops could be cut straight across, but a curve improves appearance. In any case, take the poles high enough to provide back support. Remember, however, that this is not supposed to be a lounger with the back high enough to give head support.

11. The many parts tightly bolted and nailed provide mutual support. This should be adequate in a structure of this size, but if you find that your chair seems likely to develop loose joints in the back to front direction—possibly with users tilting back onto the two back legs—you could triangulate by putting diagonals

between the legs and rails below the seat. Make the diagonals in a similar way to rails, and bolt them from near the lower rails on the rear upright to underneath the seat rails on the front uprights.

12. The wood could be left to weather to a natural greyish color, but it might be better to treat with a preservative. The posts could be given several coats of linseed oil that will finish most woods to a golden sheen. The oil takes a long time to fully dry, so the treatment should be given a long time before the chair is used.

POLE BENCH

A longer seat could be made by extending the pole chair to make it wide enough to seat two or more, but it might need stiffening and bracing. The bench shown in Fig. 4-14 is similar in many ways, but it is braced and makes more use of dowel joints. The seat area is more substantial. Some of the parts shown with dowels could be bolted if you prefer. Sizes and layout will have to be adjusted to suit materials, but the measurements shown for the chair can be used as a guide to height and width (Fig. 4-13). The length will be about 48 inches to seat two persons.

Fig. 4-14. The main parts of the bench are made from poles and the seat can be split logs.

Poles up to 3 inches in diameter are suitable. Preferably, the poles should be hardwood and they should be stripped of bark. The uprights and main lengthwise parts should be from the thicker parts of the poles, but rails and diagonals could be thinner. The seat is made up of slab offcuts from a sawmill or from split logs, possibly 5 inches or 6 inches wide.

Obtain sufficient wood, before you start making parts, so that you have enough and can match particular pieces to suit the construction. Do not use pieces with large knots, particularly for long parts, because these are weak spots.

1. Curved pieces that make a reasonable match are valuable for the rear uprights (Fig. 4-15A), but because they will be further apart, slight differences in shape will not be as apparent as in the chair. If you have to use straight pieces, assemble the ends so they slope back slightly.

2. Choose straight pieces of similar thickness for the front uprights (Fig. 4-15B). Except for the seat bearers, which should be bolted, the parts between the end uprights are all doweled.

3. Mark where the holes for dowels are to come on all legs. Make the bottom rails (Fig. 4-15C), but do not drive in the dowel ends yet.

4. Make the seat bearers (Fig. 4-15D), but do not drill them until after the rails and uprights have been finally assembled. They can have their front ends slightly higher than the rear ends.

5. Make sure the tops of the rear uprights are at the same height, and then cut the dowel ends there (Fig. 4-15E). Do the same at the front.

6. Join the uprights with their rails. See that the ends match. Drill for the bolt on the seat bearers. If their top surfaces are not level, true them with a chisel or plane.

7. Make the arms to extend forward of the front uprights a short distance, and round those projections (Fig. 4-15F). Fit their dowels into the rear uprights first, and then join the arms to the front uprights.

8. There are two lengthwise rails below seat level (Fig. 4-15G and H) and one forming the base of the back (Fig. 4-15J). These are all the same except for variations due to different wood sizes. Make these long rails, and drill the uprights for them.

9. Join the end assemblies with these lengthwise rails. As with all dowel joints, get them as tight as possible with either good drive fits or fox wedging. For further security, nails can be driven across the joints.

10. Check that the assembly, so far, stands upright on a flat surface when it is viewed from any direction.

11. The top back rail (Fig. 4-15K) looks best if curved, but it could be straight. It might be thicker than the other poles. Drill it for the rear upright dowels and fit it in position.

12. The pair of diagonal struts are there to provide lengthwise stiffness as well as for the sake of appearance (Fig. 4-15L). For greatest stiffness they should be cut to fit closely into the corners at their outer ends and should butt tightly against each other at their centers. Force the struts in when possible; secure them with nails.

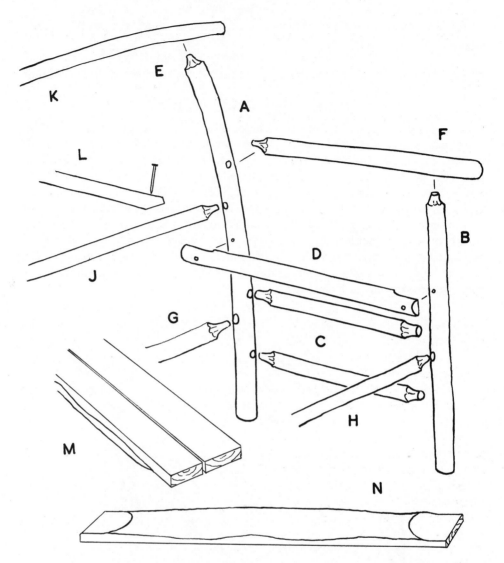

Fig. 4-15. *Bench joints are made with tapered ends fitting into holes. The seat boards are cut parallel and have their rough surfaces downward.*

13. The seat boards are made with the log section outline underneath. The tops can be left from cleaving or as sawn slabs from a log. Although they could be used with the thin edges together, it would be better to make them parallel, either completely (Fig. 4-15M) or partially, with just the greatest curves cut off. They can then be mounted almost touching, but with narrow gaps for rain to run through.

14. Prepare the undersides by paring down the ends (Fig. 4-15N) to rest on the seat bearers. Do not take the ends any thinner than essential or they will be weakened. If you have to reduce the width of a board to fit in, let the narrow

one be at the back where it takes little load. If there are variations, put the thickest board at the front. Nail the seat boards to their bearers.

15. Remove any raggedness, but sanding would be inappropriate to a rustic piece of furniture. Leave the wood bare or finish it as described for the pole chair.

PERMANENT RUSTIC TABLE

Natural poles make very good supports for a table. They could be laid together as round rods for a rather crude table top, but it is probably better to use poles for supports only, and have boards, plywood, or other smooth materials for the top. The framework could be arranged to leave outdoors so that the top lifts off and is stored under cover when not required. This table (Fig. 4-16) has a permanent top made from cleft boards or sawn slabs. It is intended to remain in one place all the year round. It might serve as a bench while working in the garden or it could be used for picnics. Sizes will depend on available materials, but a width of 24 inches or 30 inches and a length of 48 inches might be considered. The usual height for use as a bench or for sitting at with normal chairs is about 30 inches from the ground to the working surface.

Fig. 4-16. The table has its legs into the ground and the top made with pieces of log with their rough surfaces downward.

For a bench of this size, the legs and crossbars could be 3 inches or 4 inches diameter and the top could be made from split logs or slabs upwards of 6 inches wide. Construction is best done on site, with very little prefabrication, so the pieces should be too long at first to allow for cutting as they are fitted. Almost any woods can be used if they are treated with preservative.

1. Sort the pieces for the top, they settle the width you will make the table (Fig. 4-17A). Trim the edges straight and flatten the surfaces that will be on top. Leave the pieces overlength at this stage.

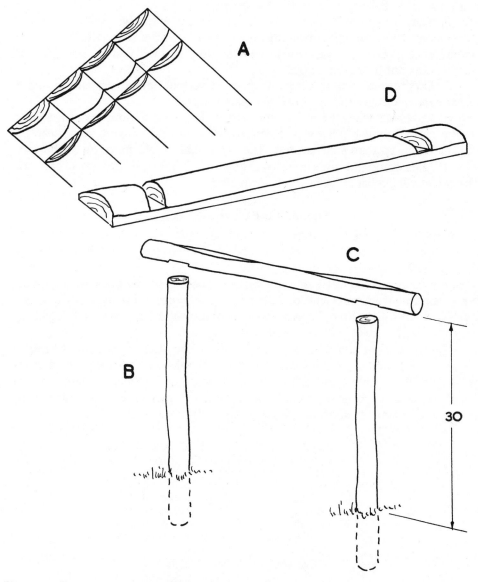

Fig. 4-17. The pieces for the tabletop are notched to fit level on the supports.

2. The supports should be about 9 inches in from what will be the ends of the table. Mark the positions on the ground. Check distances apart both ways and measure diagonals to see that the assembly is square.

3. Drive in posts (Fig. 4-17B). Measure the height you need (allowing for the crosspieces and top). Use a board with a level on it to check and mark the heights to cut off the tops of the posts.

4. Make the crosspieces (Fig. 4-17C) the same length as the width of the top. Notch them and nail them over the tops of the posts.

5. Check the flatness and level of the tops. If necessary, plane off so there is a reasonable flat top to bear the top strips.

6. Start at one side and mark one top strip with the positions of the crosspieces. Then cut and chisel out the waste so that the strip will fit over the crosspiece (Fig. 4-17D). Adjust the grooves so the strips will rest in place without rocking. Do not fix at this stage.

7. Do the same with the next strip, but you will have to adjust the depth of the grooves to get the top surfaces matching.

8. Continue across with the other strips. Regulate the depths of the slots so you get a reasonably flat top. If too much is cut out, packing pieces can be put in. When you are satisfied with the level, nail on all the parts of the top.

9. Mark across the ends and saw them level. Remove sharpness all around. The table will probably be best left untreated.

PORTABLE RUSTIC TABLE

A nonfolding portable table framework can be made from light natural poles. It could support a top made of plywood or boards held together with battens. Keep the top under cover when not in use.

Construction could be by overlapping parts, bolting them or just nailing them, but a neat construction is with doweled ends into holes in the legs. Because the legs should be thicker than the rails, the ends of the rails do not have to be reduced very much. The holes will not weaken the legs.

Choose straight poles for the top supports. The other parts do not have to be so straight, and slight twists and bends will enhance the rustic appearance (Fig. 4-18). For a table about 40 inches by 20 inches and 28 inches high, the legs could be about 2 inches in diameter and the horizontal pieces not much more than 1 inch diameter after the bark has been stripped off.

Materials List for Portable Rustic Table				
4 legs	30	×	2 diameter	
4 rails	24	×	1¼ diameter	
4 rails	38	×	1¼ diameter	
2 diagonals	30	×	1¼ diameter	
4 tops	38	×	5 × ¾	
2 battens	22	×	2 × 1	

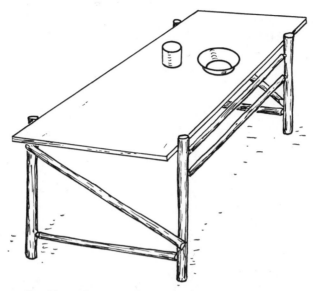

Fig. 4-18. A light rustic table can be made with parts pegged and nailed together to support a flat board top.

1. Prepare the legs first (Fig. 4-19A) by marking the positions of the holes in all of them. Remember to pair the legs. Drill through at all positions (¾ inch or ⅞ inch diameter may be suitable).

2. Make the straight pieces that will bear the top. Reduce the ends so they can go right through the holes and project slightly (Fig. 4-19B).

3. Use these as a guide to cut the lower rails (Fig. 4-19C).

4. Assemble the opposite ends while checking them for squareness and symmetry.

5. To hold the shapes, nail on diagonal struts (Fig. 4-19D). Flatten the ends slightly where they bear against the legs, but otherwise they need no special preparation. Nail through the dowels; leave them projecting slightly as a design feature or cut them off level.

6. In the long direction, the parts are held with two rails on each side (Fig. 4-19E). Make them all the same (with dowels long enough to go through and project slightly). Drill carefully and squarely so that the legs will stand upright in the finished assembly.

7. If the top is to be made of boards, they need not to be thicker than ¾ inch for the sizes suggested. Put together enough boards to make up the width, with battens underneath in positions to come just inside the bearers, so they locate the top (Fig. 4-19F). If necessary, put another batten across at the center to prevent boards warping out of line. Tongued and grooved boards would make a firmer top than plain boards.

8. If the top is a piece of plywood, fit locating battens underneath in the same way.

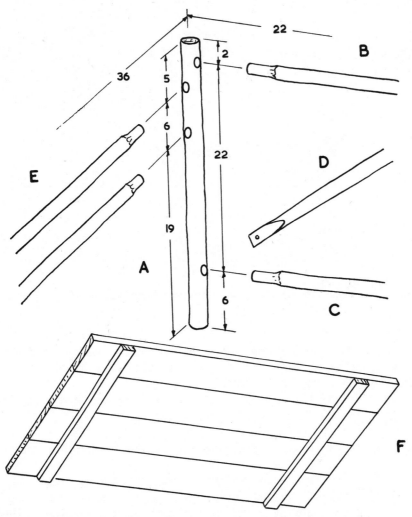

Fig. 4-19. Rails for the table frame fit into holes and the top rests on the crossbars.

GARDEN DIVIDER

An arrangement of natural poles to make an open fence between two parts of a garden will fit into most schemes better than anything more formal. The fence forms a climbing frame for roses, other flowers, or vegetables.

Although the arrangement can be quite simple (Fig. 4-20), it will fail to please the eye if posts that should be vertical are not, or rails that should be horizontal are not. If the divider comes on sloping ground, you will have to decide if the rails are to be parallel with the ground or are to be level. Posts should be upright in any case. A fence on uneven ground never looks right if it is allowed to tilt. If rails are to be horizontal, yet the ground is sloping, they will have to be arranged in step so that the rails at one level join a post nearer the ground than the next

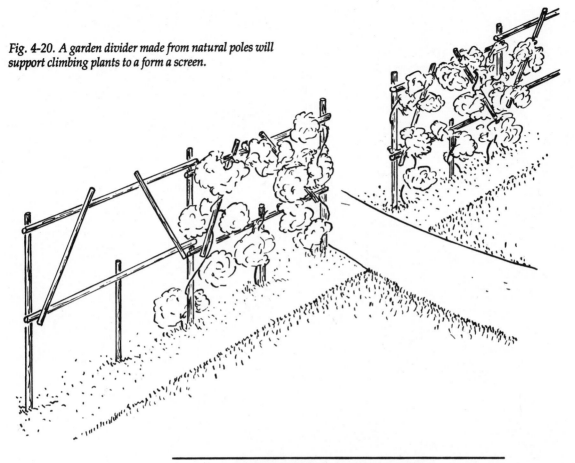

Fig. 4-20. A garden divider made from natural poles will support climbing plants to a form a screen.

Materials List for Garden Divider

6 feet high and 8 feet between posts.
All stripped fir or other straight poles

Posts	3-inch to 4-inch diameter, 96 inches long
Rails	2-inch to 3-inch diameter, 108 inches long
Diagonals	2-inch diameter, 60 inches long
Center posts	2-inch diameter, 60 inches long

---

row of rails (Fig. 4-21A). The post lengths will have to be adjusted to suit uneven ground. Aim to get the rail spacing the same in each section. Remember, it is visual effect *from a distance* that matters.

1. For a divider with a gap for a path through it to be made, lay it out first with a stretched cord (Fig. 4-21B). Mark the position of each post with a peg.

2. Prepare the posts with pointed ends and keep them slightly too long so that the tops can be leveled after driving.

3. Erect the poles while checking that they are plumb. Sight along the row as this will help you check any that are out of true with the others.

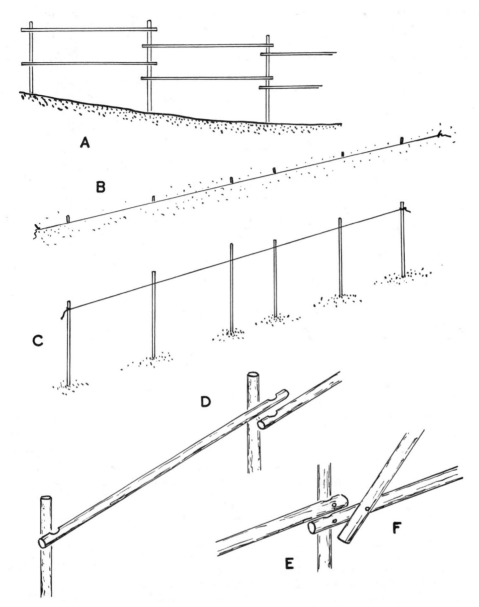

Fig. 4-21. On sloping ground, parts of a divider should be made level (A). Post positions should be kept straight (B,C). Parts can be notched and nailed or bolted together.

4. Use a cord tied to the end poles to check the levels of the tops (Fig. 4-21C), and then cut off the poles level. A sloping cut will shed water, but flat tops are common.

5. Mark the heights of rails on the posts. It is unlikely that the distances between the posts will all be the same. Work on pairs of rails in a section at one time.

6. Assuming the posts are reasonably straight, the distance between two at ground level should be the same at the top. Mark a rail at ground level and try it at the top position. If the distance there is very different, one or more posts might be out of plumb. Hollow the rail to fit around the posts (Fig. 4-21D) and nail it in position.

7. Mark the lower rail at its position, and then hollow and fit it. The rails could be cut off close to the posts, but they are shown overlapping slightly.

8. Do the same in the next section, but arrange the rails under the first ones (Fig. 4-21E). You can check proper positioning with a level. If you measure from the top of the posts, which were checked, the rails should come true. One nail through, or almost through, at each crossing should be adequate.

9. The diagonals can be lighter poles. Arrange them to overhang the rails and project upward to about the same level as the posts. One nail at each crossing should be enough (Fig. 4-21F). Their exact positioning is not important (providing you fit them in matching positions in each place).

10. A central post is recommended, and it should reach as high as the lower rail in each section. That can be driven after the other parts are erected. Much depends on what sort of climbing plants you have.

11. If you want a more closed lower section, to obscure the view or to provide more for climbing plants to cling to, use an expanding trellis.

RUSTIC PERGOLA

Natural poles make good combination with climbing flowering plants such as roses. The round rods, whether left with bark on or peeled, often look better than sawn and planed wood in support arrangements. They can be used without the same precision. If there are irregularities or differences in spacings, it is not as important as with wood cut to regular sections. You can use up pieces of poles that do not always match, and it is possible to use hammer and nail joints with success. These advantages are apparent if you make a round climbing support.

Such a pergola could be any size from about 4 feet in diameter and upward. It should usually be high enough at the eaves to walk in, and the spacing of uprights will have to suit the roses or other plants; 18 inches is about right. The example shown in Fig. 4-22 is circular, about 6 feet across, and has a conical, open roof. Diagonal pieces brace the uprights and provide something for the climbers to cling to.

The uprights are straight poles with about a 3-inch maximum diameter. Similar poles can be used for the roof, but other parts can be pieces anywhere between a 1-inch and a 3-inch diameter. All of the construction is nailed. With the interconnected parts supporting each other, this is probably strong enough. If you prefer, there could be some joints cut.

1. Mark out the circular base plan. Use a strip of wood with a spike as center and a stick scratching against the end as it is pulled round. Alternatively, use a string that is tethered to a center spike and with another at the required radius scratch the circle (Fig. 4-23A).

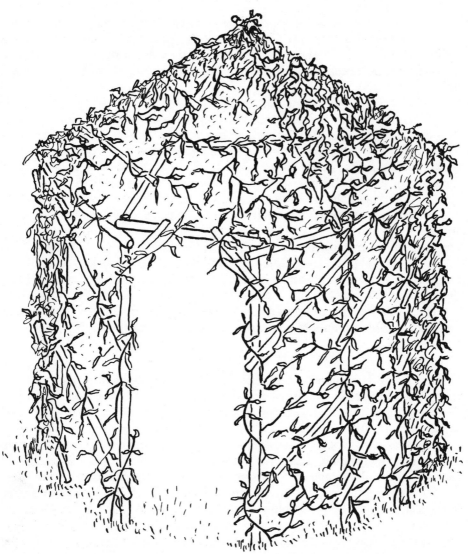

Fig. 4-22. A rustic pergola can become completely covered with a climbing plant.

2. On this circle, mark where the opening is to be. The gap can be 18 inches to 24 inches wide. Mark the positions of the other posts at about 18-inch intervals around the circle (Fig. 4-23B). Exact, even spacing is not important, but get the gaps about the same.

3. Drive the poles into the ground. There is no need to sink them to the depth they would have to be if they are to stand unaided, but get them upright and reasonably firm. Put temporary strips between them near the top (Fig. 4-23C) to hold the circle in shape.

4. Decide on the height you want the tops of the poles. Nail strips around at that level—with their ends overlapping (Fig. 4-23D)—and then cut off surplus

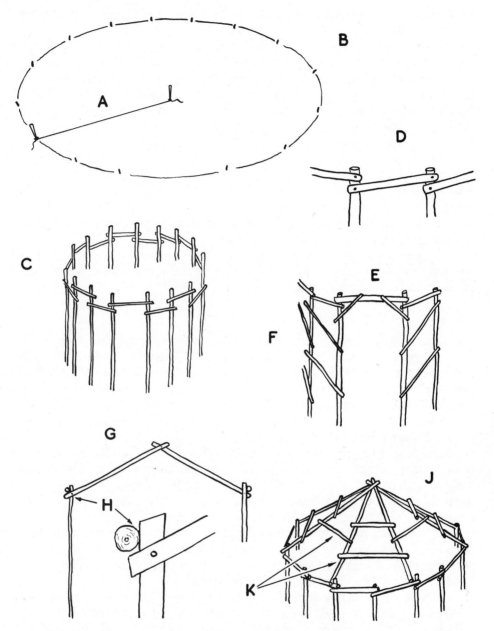

Fig. 4-23. The pergola is set out as a circle, and then it is built up around poles.

wood above these joints. The assembly should now be rigid enough for the temporary strips to be removed.

5. Put light diagonal struts at the top of the opening (Fig. 4-23E) and go round adding diagonals to the sides (Fig. 4-23F). How many and how close

depends on what you will be planting, but there should be no need to have strips closer than about 18 inches.

6. Choose two opposite uprights on which to mount a main truss. Pivot two poles together with a bolt and lift it into position so that it takes a pleasing angle (somewhere between 25 degrees and 45 degrees to horizontal), and then nail or bolt it to the posts. At the apex (Fig. 4-23G) and at the eaves (Fig. 4-23H), the ends can project slightly. Check that the assembly is put together with the rafters the same length.

7. Take other poles up the apex. There is no need to do this from every upright, but if there are about six, that should be ample. On a small-diameter pergola, four may be enough. Attach to the upright poles in the same way as the main truss, but at the apex, nail to the parts of the main truss (Fig. 4-23J) or carry one or two ends over them.

8. Unless the structure is very large, one or two strips between rafters should be enough for training flowers (Fig. 4-23K).

9. Remove raggedness at the ends. Cut off projections that might be knocked by a passing person. The wood could be treated with preservative, but it would be satisfactory if left in its natural state.

SIMPLE ARCH

An arch can stand anywhere on a path and provide a decorative feature with its climbing flowers or foliage. Its standard place, however, is at a division between parts of a garden. An arch can stand independently or it could be combined with a garden divider or fence. In that case, it can be simply made by carrying the divider end posts upward to support a shaped top, without doubling the posts or extending the thickness of the arch. If a broader arch is required, a suitable design is shown in the next project.

For a simple, single-pole-thickness arch, the uprights can be the end posts of the garden divider. If the arch is to stand unaided, get stout poles into the ground (with struts if necessary). The project is a basic design (Fig. 4-24). All of the parts should be poles stripped of bark, and preferably at least partly seasoned so that they do not crack after being erected for a while.

1. Make the poles long enough to give clearance under the crossbar for anyone walking through even when there is trailing foliage. That means about 84 inches above the ground and probably 18 inches into the ground (Fig. 4-25A). Thickness should be about about 3 inches or more.

2. Make the crossbar about the same diameter as the tops of the posts, or a little more, so as to cover the end grain and prevent rain from entering and causing rot. The bar can be notched to go over the flat post tops (Fig. 4-25B) or V notches can be used (Fig. 4-25C). In either case, drive nails downward into the posts.

3. If you want a ranch-style arch to serve as an entrance, with a hanging board carrying a name, a section cut diagonally across a log (Fig. 4-25D) would make a suitable name board. Hang it with chain or wire and make the assembly high enough for the board to clear heads.

Fig. 4-24. A simple arch can form a gap in a fence.

4. For the more usual pointed arch, make two pieces that can be nailed or bolted to the posts and crossbar (Fig. 4-25E). This type of corner provides stiffness for the structure by triangulating. Make sure the nails or bolts are secure. At the top, the two pieces meet (Fig. 4-25F) with nails between them and a small brace across, or they can be notched into each other and allowed to extend slightly (Fig. 4-25G). There is no need to take the notches to half thickness; enough to flatten the meeting surfaces is all that is necessary.

5. If you have doubts about the rigidity of poles into the ground with no other support, you can add diagonal struts. Much depends on the soil. Sinking

the posts into concrete would be the most rigid structure. If the struts are to be fitted, it will probably be satisfactory to drive them in at about 45 degress (Fig. 4-25H). Cut them too long and drive until they become secure, and then cut off and bolt or nail to the posts (Fig. 4-25). It should be sufficient to do this one way only, but they can be in both directions with the tops overlapping.

6. Many plants will climb almost anything, whether it is smooth or rough, but peeled poles can be fairly slippery. If your plants need help, there could be short pieces of wood nailed to the outsides of the posts to prevent turns of the

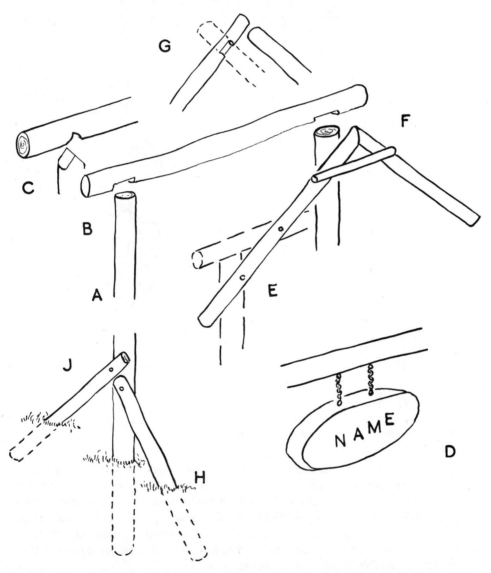

Fig. 4-25. The simple arch can have its parts notched together. Struts will be needed to the ground. A hanging name board might be appropriate.

plants slipping down. Less obvious would be a few nails driven so that about ½ inch of the heads project.

DOUBLE ARCH

An arch based on four posts can be given thickness, and the plants climbing over it will make a more impressive display than they could on a simple two-post arch. How thick you make it depends on needs and the situation, but an arch of normal size might be 18 inches thick. It would be less attractive if made rather thin; 12 inches ought to be regarded as the minimum for most double arches. In some situations, you might want to give more of a tunnel effect, and the arch could be 36 inches or more thick.

As shown in Fig. 4-26, the arch is assumed to be about 84 inches under the crossbar, about 48 inches wide, and 18 inches thick. For that size, the posts could

Fig. 4-26. A double arch with its uprights in the ground is strong enough to stand unaided, and it forms a good base for climbers.

be 2 inches or 3 inches thick and the other parts thinner. Much depends on the type of wood. The diagonals need not be much more than 1 inch thick (providing they are without flaws). All of the wood should be stripped of bark (unless the bark is very tight), and it should at least be partially seasoned.

1. Select the wood for its locations. The main structures are made up of posts with the crossbars and rafters bolted through. Choose the best wood for these parts.

2. Lay a pair of posts flat on the ground with their tops square to each other and put a pair of rafters over them so as to mark the angle the posts tops are to be cut. The exact angles are not important, but rafters at 25 degrees to 35 degrees to horizontal will be about right. From this trial assembly, you can mark the lengths of the rafters.

3. Cut the back of the top of each post with a notch to take the end of the crossbar, which will be flattened to fit (Fig. 4-27A). Cut a notch at the front. It will not matter if the cut is square across, but it will look better if it is about the angle of the rafter (Fig. 4-27B). Do not cut away the posts too much; there should be about half thickness left at the center. The tops of the posts can be pointed for appearance and to shed rain water.

4. Mark the positions of the posts on the ground. Besides being the correct distance apart, check that they re square by measuring diagonals. Erect the posts while checking that tops are level.

5. Make the crossbars (with flats at the ends). Drill them and the posts for bolts (Fig. 4-27C). Put the bolts in with their ends extending outward.

6. Make the rafters. At the tops, notch each pair into each other (Fig. 4-27D) and bolt through. Check that the distance between bolt holes will be the same each side, and then drill and bolt to the posts.

7. The two assemblies have to be linked with short pieces. Put the first at the apex, resting in the V of the rafters (Fig. 4-27E), and nail it in place. This should steady the assembly.

8. Put more pieces on the rafters above the posts joints (Fig. 4-27F). Check that the assembly has not gone out of square by seeing that these pieces are the same length.

9. There could be two more pieces put across just below the crossbar joints (Fig. 4-27G).

10. What other pieces are put across depend on the the pattern of climbing plants you hope to arrange. There could be another piece across level near the ground and one halfway, at each side, and then diagonals between them (Fig. 4-27H). Some of these could be merely nailed on without preparation, but the nailed joints are better if the ends of the pieces are flattened slightly where they contact the posts. Of course, the pieces brace the whole assembly, but only a few are needed for stiffening and the main concern is to provide places for climbers to grip.

11. Put a few more cross pieces on the rafters (Fig. 4-27) and diagonals if you prefer. To get the plants to provide a good coverage at the top, closer supports are needed than on the vertical sides.

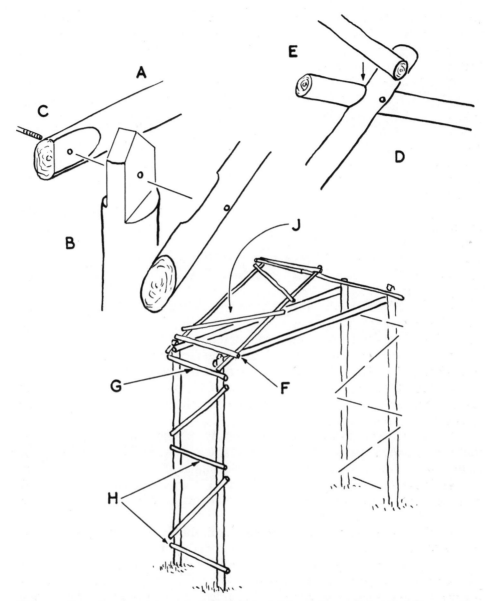

Fig. 4-27. The main parts of the arch should be bolted. Diagonal braces help to keep the assembly in shape.

12. If the posts have a good grip in the ground, the whole arch should be very firm and rigid. If necessary, diagonal struts could be taken outward near the base.

5
CHAPTER

Seats

Seats of various sorts are the most common outdoor furniture. There is a place in a garden for more formal furniture that is made from wood sawn to thickness and usually to width as well. If it is planed, the furniture can be given a painted or varnished finish. Such furniture is durable and good looking in a planned garden with paths and lawns. Rustic seats and other furniture are more appropriate to natural surroundings.

Furniture of this sort is of a standard better than hammer-and-nail construction. Although the work might not be in the same class as cabinetry for indoor use, many of the same joints and techniques should be used. A few parts can be nailed, but where nails might be used in cruder construction it is more common to have screws. Mortise and tenon joints have more uses, but dowels can be substituted for many of them.

For this sort of furniture, the wood chosen should be of reasonable quality. It could be softwood. Many of the pines and firs that are resinous and with fairly straight grain are suitable. Hardwood should be more durable and some very longlasting outdoor furniture is made of oak and teak. Most planed wood can be used in stock sizes. Allow for it being at least ⅛ inch less than the specified size (before planing).

There is not much use for plywood, but is can be built into table tops and other areas where a large, clean expanse is needed. It should be exterior or marine quality and preferably framed around the edges with glued strips that prevent moisture getting into the edges of the veneers.

If you will be cutting joints and using glue in them, the wood should be dry. If parts are only nailed or screwed, it is not so important that the wood is fully seasoned. Glue will not hold properly if there is excess moisture in the wood, and joints that are made tight at first might open as the wood dries out. If you obtain wood already cut and planed from a lumberyard, it should have been seasoned. It is advisable to get it ahead of your needs and keep it for at least a few weeks before working on it.

In general, do not to mix woods in construction, but you make a framework of hardwood and fit slats for seat and back, for instance, made from softwood. Parts that are in contact with the ground are the first to develop rot. Oak and some other hardwoods have a better resistance to rot than softwoods. Keep in mind that wood can be treated with a preservative. If you are planning a painted finish, make sure the preservative is suitable for use below paint.

STOOL

There are many uses for a stool in your garden and yard. It is something steady to stand on to gain height, and it can be used for sitting by children. You will be glad to have a low seat as an alternative to bending or stooping when dealing with garden chores (Fig. 5-1). Two identical stools can be used with a plank across for working or sitting.

Fig. 5-1. A simple stool has many uses in a garden and yard.

Materials List for Stool						
2 legs	12	×	7	×	¾
2 sides	18	×	3	×	¾
1 top	18	×	7	×	¾

The wood suggested is all the same section; for this stool it is 7 inches wide and ¾ inch thick, before planing. The same method can be used for stools or benches of other sizes.

1. Make a drawing of one end to get the length and angle of the leg (Fig. 5-2A). For stability, the bottom of the leg should come below the end of the stool top.

2. Mark out and cut the two legs (Fig. 5-2B). The angles at the top, bottom, and notches should be the same angle as on the preliminary drawing. The V cutout is made toward a hole to reduce the risk of a split developing.

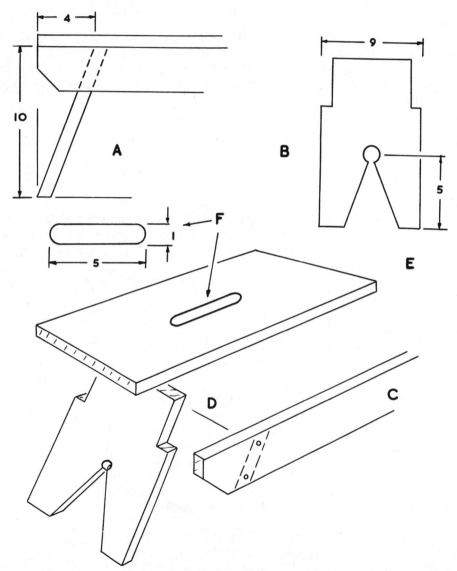

Fig. 5-2. The stool has feet angled to give stability. A slot in the top provides a hand grip for lifting.

3. Cut a piece down the middle to make the two sides (Fig. 5-2C). Bevel the ends and mark where the legs will come. Drill for two screws at each position.

4. Join the sides to the legs (Fig. 5-2D), preferably with waterproof glue as well as screws. Brass or galvanized steel screws should be used. An exception is if the stool will be kept under cover most of the time. In that case, plain steel screws might be good enough. Check squareness of the assembly when viewed from above, and the levelness of the legs on a flat surface. If there is a tendency to twist, leave the assembly for the glue to set with a weight on top.

5. Make a top to glue and screw on (Fig. 5-2E). The hand hole at the center is useful for picking up and carrying (Fig. 5-2F).

BENCH

A bench could be made like a large stool, but as you design higher and longer, for the sake of stability, it becomes advisable to provide a wider spread to the feet. That could be done by sloping the sides of the stool legs, but the bench shown in Fig. 5-3 has a different method of construction. Stiffness and strength are provided by a central piece of 2-inch-×-4-inch wood under the top (instead of the pair of pieces at the sides).

1. Set out the intended end view (Fig. 5-4A) in order to get the leg length and angle for cutting joints.

2. Make the two legs, but do not cut the top slots yet (Fig. 5-4B). They taper to the top, but the bottom is cut with a V into a hole. The top and bottom should be made to the angles found in the preliminary drawing.

3. Cut the center rib to length. Check that it has a flat top surface to fit against the bench top. Mark on it the angles the legs are to be and the depths of grooves that will leave about 1 inch solid wood at the center (Fig. 5-4C). The groove widths should be a close fit on the legs.

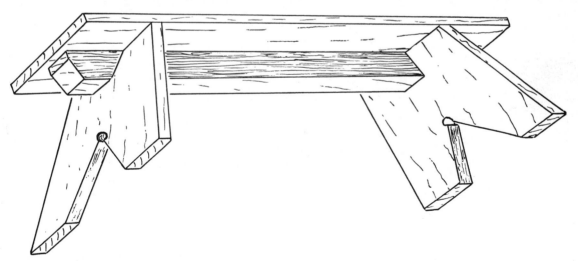

Fig. 5-3. This bench has a central stiffening member.

Materials List for Bench

1 top	48 × 9 × 1¼
1 rib	48 × 4 × 2
2 legs	18 × 12 × 1¼

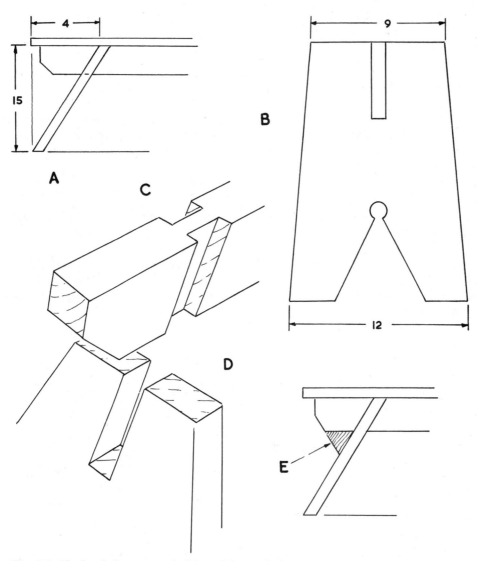

Fig. 5-4. The bench legs are notched into the central piece.

4. Mark the widths of the grooves in the tops of the legs and angle both the tops of the legs and the bottoms of the grooves to suit (Fig. 5-4D). Leave a little extra length on the tops of the legs to plane level after assembly.

5. Drive in and glue the legs to the rib. With many woods and firm joints this should be all the construction necessary, but if the fit of the joints is not as good as you wish or you have doubts about the strength of the wood, there could be stiffening blocks glued and screwed between the parts (Fig. 5-4E).

6. The top is a plain board and has rounded corners and edges. Use glue and screw it downward into the central rib and the tops of the legs. If you prefer not to have screw heads showing on top, they could be counterbored and have wood plugs glued over them. An alternative is to use dowels instead of screws. Screws or dowels located near the edges of the legs are important to make a close, firm joint.

TENONED BENCH

If you have quite thick slabs of wood available, they can be made into a substantial bench (Fig. 5-5). It will be heavy but in a garden that can be an advantage. The bench is unlikely to tip over and others are less likely to move it from where you want it to stay. Thicker wood is less liable to be affected by exposure to all kinds of weather. There is more labor in working the thick wood, but the techniques are simple.

The wood suggested could be as converted in a sawmill with little further treatment before you start on it. It does not have to be planed. The sections to look for are about 12 inches wide and 2 inches thick. They could be greater, but

Fig. 5-5. A heavy bench is useful to work on as well as to sit on.

Approximate sizes

1 top	60 × 12 × 2
2 legs	60 × 12 × 2

very much thinner would not be strong enough without additional bracing. The wood may have waney, or diminished, edges, but they would have to be eased to allow for users sitting without sharp or rough edges touching their legs. That could be done without destroying the character of the waney edging.

1. Prepare the top piece of wood. If it has a straight edge, you can mark out squarely from that. If there are waney edges on both sides, it would be better to draw a centerline and mark out the joints squarely from that.

2. Decide on the height and draw the angle of the leg at one end (Fig. 5-6A). Set an adjustable bevel to that and keep it at that setting for all marking of the joints (Fig. 5-6B).

3. Cut the wood for the legs, but leave the pieces slightly overlength at this stage.

4. Scheme the joints so the tenons are about square in section and the gaps between are about the same. It is better to set the tenons in from the edge than to make open mortises there. Mark the chosen spacing across the top of one leg (Fig. 5-6C) and use that as a guide for marking other positions.

5. Mark out the mortises (Fig. 5-6D) in each position and the tenons on the tops of the legs (Fig. 5-6E). Use the adjustable bevel to transfer markings to the correct positions on opposite sides. Allow for the tenons being too long when you cut them so that they can be planed level after assembly.

6. Cut the joints. Much of the work on the tenons can be done with a saw, but the angled bottoms of the legs will have to be cut with a chisel. Some of the waste in the mortises can be drilled out, but because of the angles final shaping must be done with a chisel.

7. When you are satisfied with the joint cutting, mark the lengths of the legs, including the angles at the bottom. Check them against each other. The bottom of each could be a V cut, but it is shown scooped to a curve (Fig. 5-6F). The legs are shown parallel, but they could be broadened toward the bottom for increased stability.

8. It might be sufficient to drive in the tenons, with or without glue, but for long-term security it is advisable to use wedges. Make saw cuts in the ends of the tenons before assembly. These could be straight across (Fig. 5-6G), but they will make an interesting pattern if driven diagonally (Fig. 5-6H). All the wedges at one end could be same way or you could alternate the angles or pair them if there is an even number of tenon ends to be dealt with. Before wedging, make sure all tenons are driven in as tightly as possible. Level the tops of the tenons and wedges to complete the bench.

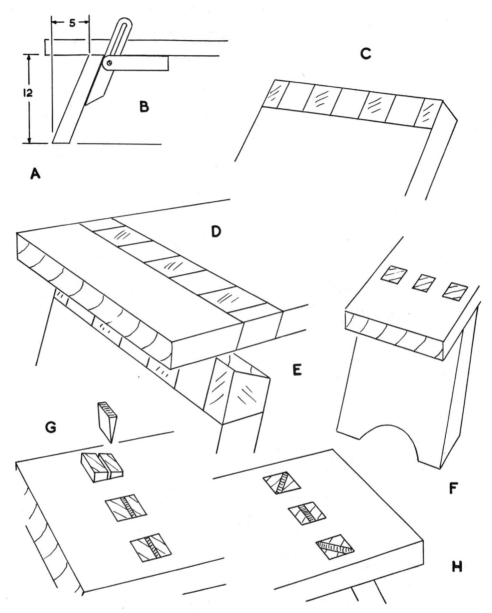

Fig. 5-6. The splayed legs are tenoned into the top and can be wedged.

PLAIN BENCH WITH BACKREST

A seat without a backrest might be a welcome sight when you need a brief rest, but if you want to sit for long you need support for your back. There are various degrees of complication in seats with backrests, but the example shown in Fig. 5-7 is simple in appearance and construction. In addition, it can offer reasonable comfort to tired bodies.

Fig. 5-7. A backrest increases the comfort of a bench.

Materials List for Plain Bench with Backrest

2 legs	15	×	12	×	1¼
2 seat supports	14	×	2	×	1¼
2 feet	18	×	3	×	1¼
4 pads	4	×	4	×	1¼
2 backrest supports	30	×	3	×	1¼
1 seat	72	×	14	×	1¼
1 backrest	72	×	6	×	1¼
1 rail	70	×	5	×	1¼

Most of the construction is with screws, but the lengthwise stiffening rail has mortise and tenon joints at the ends. The material is planed wood, which may be a softwood finished with paint, or a durable hardwood could be left untreated. Sizes can be varied, but a top 14 inches wide is suggested at a comfortable height for sitting. The rear support is at a height and angle that should suit most users.

How long to make the bench will have to be decided in relation to the available space and what wood you have, but a length of 6 feet will suit three people or even four for a short time.

1. Sort the available wood and relate it to an end view, which will control most sizes (Fig. 5-8A). Make a full-size drawing. Have the seat at a comfortable height and locate the backrest in relation to it. A slop of about 10 degrees from vertical will give a suitable angle for comfort and for attaching to the ends without reducing the useful width of the seat (Fig. 5-8B). To allow for the need for resistance against tipping back, draw the feet further back than forward of the end (Fig. 5-8C).

2. The ends could be tenoned into the seat supports and the feet, but they are shown overlapped and glued and screwed. Make the pair of ends carefully squared and mark where the rail will come (Fig. 5-8D).

3. Make the rail and cut tenons at its ends. They are the full thickness of the wood, but cut down to shoulders. If the tenons are a little more than half the total width of the rail, that will be right. Cut the mortises and tenons, but do not assemble these parts yet.

4. Glue and screw on crossbars on the upper surfaces at the tops of the legs (Fig. 5-8E), extending forward to support the seat.

5. Make the feet (Fig. 5-8F) and attach them to the outsides of the bottoms of the legs. Put pads under the feet (Fig. 12-8G). Make the pads wide enough to extend outward a little and come under the thickness of the legs. Check that the two legs match as a pair.

6. Make the backrest supports (Fig. 5-8H). Let the bottom of the support come close against its foot. At the top, cut away to let the backrest strip fit in. Round the top corners and take off the sharpness of all exposed parts. Glue and screw to the legs while checking that the two ends match.

7. Fit the rail to the legs. Put saw cuts across the ends of the tenons before assembly. Glue in the tenons and spread them with wedges. When the glue has set, level the tenon ends with the leg surfaces.

8. Make the seat (Fig. 5-8J). If you have to join boards to make up the width, they could have plain glued edges, be tongued and grooved, or there could be cleats across underneath. At the ends, allow the seat to project a short distance past the backrest supports around which they are notched (Fig. 5-8K). Round the extending corners and the front edge. Fit the seat by screwing into the supports and the tops of the legs. This will look best if the screws are counterbored and covered with wood plugs. Assemble on a flat surface and see that the seat will stand without wobbling.

9. Make the backrest (Fig. 5-8L). Let its ends extend the same amount as the seat. Round the corners and well round the front edges. Join to the supports with counterbored screws, in the same way as the seat.

10. There will probably be no need to sand the seat, but make sure there is no roughness left before painting or applying other finish.

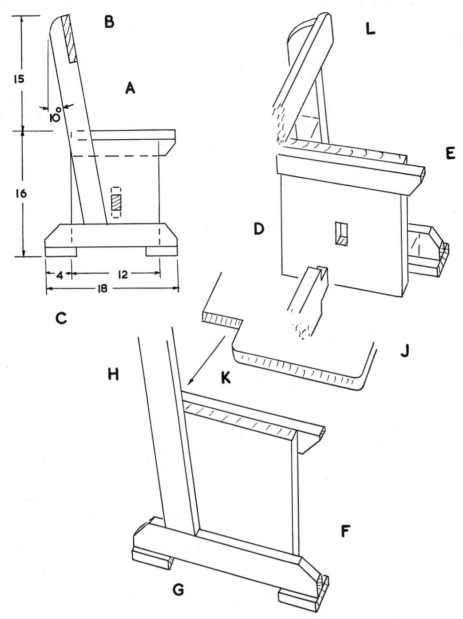

Fig. 5-8. *The backrest is at a slight angle. Most joints are nailed, but the bottom rail is better tenoned.*

BENCH WITH SHAPED SEAT

A flat seat becomes uncomfortable after a while. One with a hollow back-to -front seat is easier to sit on for a long period. A hollow can be arranged with a number of strips that run lengthwise instead of a single board. The lengthwise pieces can be of light section with frequent supports, or they can be stouter pieces that are

Fig. 5-9. A shaped seat is more comfortable than a flat one.

Materials List for Bench with Shaped Seat

4 frame pieces	24 × 4 × 2
4 frame pieces	16 × 4 × 2
2 backrest supports	34 × 4 × 2
1 backrest	72 × 4 × 2
4 seat pieces	72 × 4 × 2
1 front rail	60 × 4 × 2
2 struts	24 × 4 × 2

strong enough in themselves. See Fig. 5-9. The method can be used for a bench of almost any length if supports are arranged not more than 60 inches apart. Here it is assumed that the bench is about 6 feet long and with two supports.

Although various sizes of wood can be used, it is suggested that all parts of this bench be made of 2-inch-×-4-inch standard sections. In some situations, the wood need not be planed. For good construction and a painted finish, it is better to have planed wood. It will not matter if there are a few small knots in the smaller support parts, but the lengthwise seat and back slats should be as clear of flaws as possible.

The support frames are made with halving joints. Other parts are held with screws and the back supports are bolted to the frames. The stout sections joined together will product considerable mutual support, but it is in the length that the benches often begin to become slack. This bench is braced with diagonal struts at the front.

1. Prepare the wood for the two frames. Check its width and use this information when making a full-size drawing of an end view (Fig. 5-10A). Start by drawing a line to represent the floor and another square to it for the bench front. Draw a line parallel to the floor 14 inches up and, on this line, measure 22 inches from the front to join at a slope to a point 24 inches from the front on the floor line. That gives your basic outline on which the other parts are drawn.

2. The pair of top pieces should be hollowed (Fig. 5-10B). Mark the width of the curve and its depth, and then spring a flexible piece of wood through the points so that you can pencil a curve.

3. So the bottom of each frame only stands at its ends, and is less liable to rock on uneven ground, mark similar curves in the bottom pieces (Fig. 5-10C).

4. From the full-size layout, mark and cut the parts of each frame (Fig. 5-10D). Cut back the top part at the front by the thickness of the front rail (Fig. 5-10E). Make a pair of frames with the joints glued and screwed.

5. Make the two backrest supports. They cross over the frame parts and will be bolted through (Fig. 5-10F). At the top, the backrest could be let in level, but it would be more comfortable if the notch is made so it comes at a slightly more upright angle (Fig. 5-10G).

6. Cut the bottoms of the backrest supports to match the bottom curve. Coat the meeting surfaces with preservative, if you are not gluing them, and bolt the supports to the outsides of the frames.

7. Have the four pieces ready for the seat. Drill them for counterbored screws into the frames (which will come about 9 inches in from the ends). Round all exposed edges and ends.

8. Make the front rail to fit into the notches in the frames (Fig. 5-10H). Screw it in place and immediately screw on the seat pieces so that the assembly is held rigidly. Check squareness as you assemble and see that the frames will be upright. Work where you can stand back and view the bench from many directions.

9. Add the backrest (Fig. 5-10J). It should be the same length as the seat parts and it should be well rounded on the front edges and ends. Check that the backrest is level and the supports are upright when viewed from the front. Attach it with counterbored and plugged screws.

10. Make the diagonal struts at the front (Fig. 5-10K). They should be at about 45 degrees. Fit them behind the front rail (with bolts through). At their lower ends screw them into the frames.

11. Remove any roughness and finish the bench with paint or preservative.

CHAIRS

A chair could be made like a bench, but kept short enough to seat only one person. If all that is required is a stool, any of the bench designs could be made short

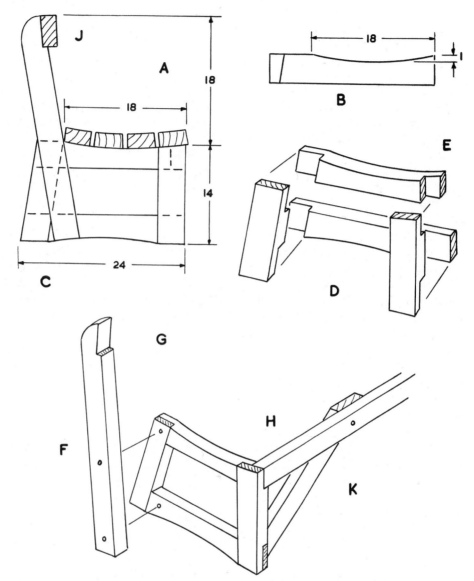

Fig. 5-10. The parts of the substantial assembly are mostly halved together and bolted.

and without a back. A short bench would make a satisfactory seat (with the same limitations of comfort as if made longer).

Individual garden seats are usually expected to be more comfortable and have wider seats for two or more people. They are generally too elaborate to be called benches. Arms are often included in these single or multiple seats. Besides their obvious additional comfort, they have a structural advantage. With the lengthening of the front legs and the arm framing, there is extra bracing involved that stiffens the chair. This provides better resistance to the sitter who tilts it back or sideways.

FLAT STRIP ARMCHAIR

Although some of the better armchairs for use outdoors have joints very similar to indoor furniture, it is possible to make a satisfactory chair with flat strips and most joints screwed. They could be nailed, but it is better to use glue and screws to make a durable chair that will stand up to exposure.

All of the parts of this chair (Fig. 5-11) can be strips of the same section. However, there would be an advantage in making the four legs thicker. Although the parts of the chair are square with each other, the back support slopes and your posture when sitting should be comfortable (although it's obviously not a lounging chair).

This is a good project for a first attempt at chairmaking. It is also a suitable project for a short run of quantity production either because you need several chairs or because you want to sell some. The parts are without angles to cut and fit. Therefore, a series of each part for many chairs can be prefabricated successfully. Even if you are only making one chair, prepare all parts that should match at the same time so that relevant measurements are the same. For instance,

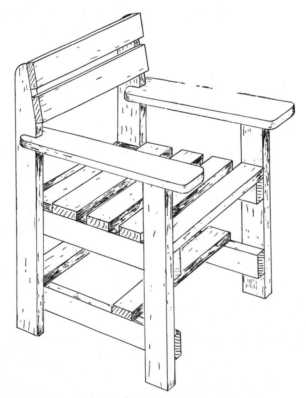

Fig. 5-11. A strong chair is suitable for leaving outside in all weather.

Materials List for Strip Armchair

2 rear legs	32 × 3 × 1
2 front legs	24 × 3 × 1
2 seat rails	20 × 3 × 1
2 bottom rails	20 × 3 × 1
2 arms	21 × 3 × 1
4 seat strips	20 × 3 × 1
3 crosswire strips	20 × 3 × 1
2 backrests	22 × 3 × 1

the front and back legs are different lengths, but many of the markings on them have to be the same distance from the bottom.

1. There is no need to make a full-size drawing because no bevels or shapings are involved, but study the side view (Fig. 5-12A) so that you understand the sizes and relationships of parts to each other.

2. Mark out the front and rear legs (Fig. 5-12B), showing the positions of the parts that will be attached to them. Allow a little extra at the top of the front legs at this stage. Mark a taper from just above where the arm will come on the rear leg. Taking it 1 inch back from the edge should be about right. If you leave fitting the backrest pieces until after the chair has been partly assembled, you can check the slope against your back and increase it if necessary before finishing the chair.

3. Prepare the pieces that go from back to front at each side. The bottom rail (Fig. 5-12C) is a plain piece of wood with the locations of the crosswise strips marked on it (Fig. 5-13A). The seat rail is similar, but it is cut back by the thickness of the rear crosswire strip (Figs. 5-12D and 5-13B). Cut the arms (Fig. 5-12E) to length, but leave further work on them until later.

4. The four seat pieces and the three crosswise strips (Fig. 5-12F) are all plain strips 20 inches long that fit on the seat rails (Fig. 5-13C) and the bottom rails (Fig. 5-13D).

5. Square off the tops of the front legs. Well round the edges and corners of the arms (Figs. 5-12E and 5-13E). Where the arm will connect to its rear leg, make a shallow notch (Fig. 5-12G) and cut the end of the arm to engage with it (Fig. 5-12H).

6. Start assembling the ends by joining the legs with the seat and lower rails. It is advisable to use waterproof glue in the joints. It should be sufficient to then use three screws in each crossing (Fig. 5-12J). Check squareness and make sure opposite ends make a pair.

7. Fit the arms. If the joints to the rear legs make a good fit, it should be sufficient to only glue them, but extra strength can come from a long screw driven across each joint. At the front legs the arms can be screwed down into the tops of the legs. Because this is end grain, it will help to drill across for dowels so part of the screw thread can go through them for a stronger grip (Fig. 5-12K). The screw heads should be counterbored and plugged for a better appearance.

8. Join the crosspieces to the bottom rail and to the rear ends of the seat rails. Check squareness with the chair standing on a level surface. Fit the four

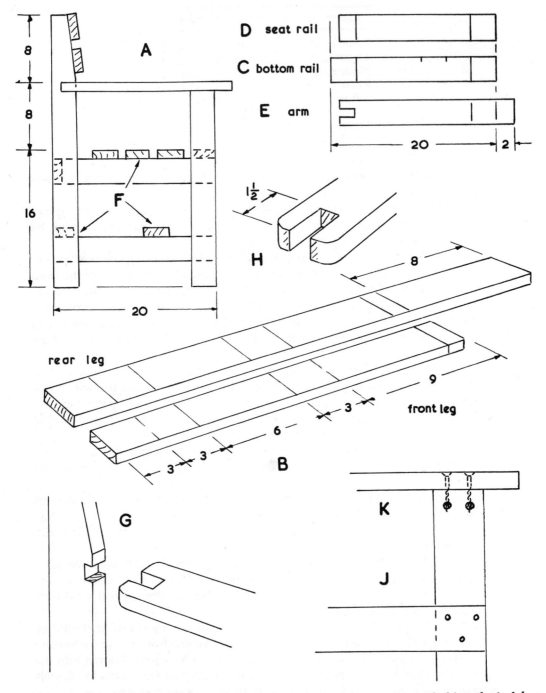

D seat rail

C bottom rail

E arm

A

F

H

1½

rear leg

8

9

3

front leg

6

3 — 3

B

G

K

J

8

8

16

20

20 — 2

Fig. 5-12. The chair parts overlap and are glued and screwed, but the arms are notched into the back legs.

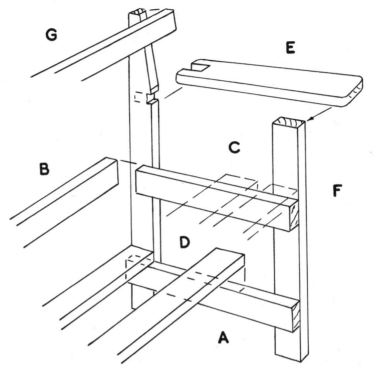

Fig. 5-13. Showing the relative positions of the chair parts.

seat pieces to their rails (Fig. 5-13F) after rounding their top edges. Have one rail level with the front legs. Gaps about 1 inch between the strips should give you a suitable spread. All of these joints can be made with glue and two long screws.

9. The backrest pieces are shown with their ends level with the legs, but they could be allowed to overlap with rounded corners. Round the exposed edges in any case and attach them to the legs (Fig. 5-13G). The tops of the rear legs can be left square or rounded to blend into the top backrest strips.

10. Remove any roughness and finish the wood with paint or preservative.

FLAT STRIP BENCH

The flat strip armchair can be extended to make a seat for two or more. A few modifications are needed to give it the extra strength needed to allow for the greater weight and possible movements of the users. This has to be mainly stiffness rather than heaviness. A bench 48 inches long (Fig. 5-14) can be made stronger by using legs of greater section, notching parts together instead of relying only on surface joints, and providing some diagonal bracing under the seat. The drawings also allow for the seat sloping back slightly to give a little more comfort than a flat seat.

The parts could be all softwood and painted. Oak or other hardwood will be both more durable and perhaps better suited to a garden situation. In any case, the wood should be machined to size, planed all round, and reasonably free from

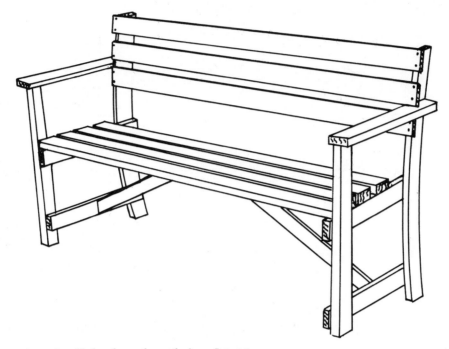

Fig. 5-14. A comfortable bench can be made from flat strips.

Materials List for Flat Strip Bench						
2 rear legs	32	×	2½	×	2½	
2 front legs	25	×	2½	×	2½	
2 seat rails	20	×	3	×	1	
2 bottom rails	19	×	3	×	1	
2 arms	22	×	3	×	1	
1 seat rail	48	×	3	×	1	
4 seat slats	50	×	3	×	1	
2 backrest slats	50	×	3	×	1	
1 seat cleat	16	×	3	×	1	
2 struts	30	×	3	×	1	
2 rear leg caps	4½	×	4½	×	1	

knots or other flaws (particularly in the long parts). Joints should be made with waterproof glue and screws.

1. The side view of Fig. 5-15A gives the main dimensions. There is no need to draw all this full size, but you should draw the outlines of the legs up to the seat level and put the sloping lines across for the angled cuts that will have to be made for the seat rails (Fig. 5-15B). All other marking out and cuts will be square, so you can measure them directly on the wood.

2. Mark out the rear legs (Fig. 5-16A). Get the widths of the slots by measuring the wood that has to fit them. It will probably be less than its nominal dimension and it helps to make all joints tight fits. Notches need not be more

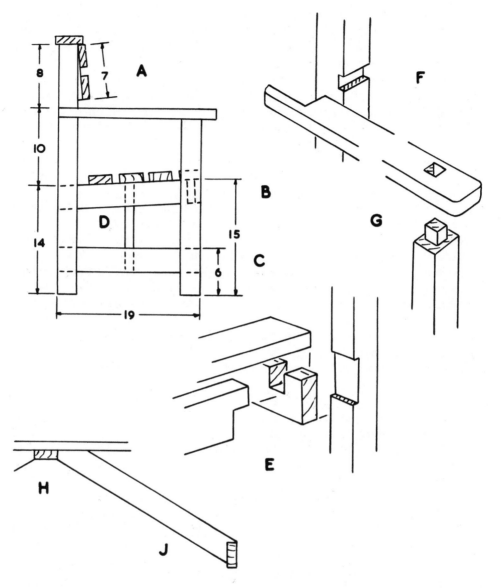

Fig. 5-15. Suitable sizes for the bench (A-D), leg and rail joints (E), arm joints (F,G) and bracing (H,J).

than ¼ inch deep. Their purpose is to provide location and resistance to movement; screws provide strength. Cut the notches to make a pair of legs.

3. At the top of each leg, add the pieces that give slope to the backrest strips (Fig. 5-16B). They taper from 1 inch to almost a feather edge.

4. Mark out the front legs (Fig. 5-16C). Although the seat slopes the armrests are level. Leave some excess length for cutting the tenon flush with the top of its armrest after fitting. Cut the notches in a similar way to those on the rear legs in order to make a pair of legs.

5. Prepare the bottom rails (Fig. 5-15C and 5-16D) that go straight across. Prepare the seat rails (Figs. 5-15D and 5-16E), which are similar but allow for the slight slope and at the forward ends they have to be notched to take the lengthwise rail under the front seat slat (Figs. 5-15E and 5-16F).

6. The armrests extend forward of the front legs by 2 inches. At the rear legs, their inner surfaces come level with the insides of the rear legs, and then they go into the notches and extend outside the legs (Fig. 5-15F). At the front, they could be screwed downward in the same way as in the previous project. With the thicker legs, however, it is better to use mortise and tenon joints. Mark the joints so the inner surface of an arm comes level with the leg. Cut the tenons back a little all round (Figs. 5-15G and 5-16G). Put saw cuts across the tenons so wedges can be used during assembly.

7. The two end frameworks can now be assembled. Three or four screws and glue in each joint should be adequate. Check that the legs are parallel and the bottom rails are square to them. Fit the rails first and then add the armrests. At the rear legs, screws through the extending part will supplement glue in the slot. Well round the exposed edges and corners of the arms. At the front legs, glue the tenons tight and drive in wedges. Leave the glue to set, and then level the tops of the tenons. See that the two frameworks match as a pair and are without twist.

8. Make the front rail so that it is notched to fit into the seat rails (Figs. 5-15E and 5-16F). Check that it is straight, this is particularly important along its top surface where it has to be under the front seat slat. Lack of straightness there would be very obvious in the finished bench.

9. Prepare the materials for the backrest and the seat slats. These should have rounded edges to the front and top. The seat slats should finish level with the outsides of their rails or they could extend a short distance and be rounded. The front slat has to be cut back to fit between the front legs. The backrest slats might also be cut level with the legs or extended and rounded. Drill all these parts for two screws at each crossing.

10. To get the bench assembled squarely, first fit the front rail, a seat slat near the back, and the top backrest slat. These three will hold the assembly while you check squareness by measuring diagonals. When you are satisfied with squareness, fit the other lengthwise parts. Screw the front slat to its rail.

11. Turn the bench over. At the center of the seat slats, put a cleat piece across underneath (Fig. 5-15H) to join the slats together and provide stiffness.

12. At the center of the third seat slat from the front, make diagonal struts to the bottom end rails (Fig. 5-15J). Cut the bottoms of the struts to fit over the rails (Fig. 5-16H). These struts are to provide resistance to lengthwise movement in the assembly and should be a close fit at each end (with screws to hold them in place).

13. The tops of the rear legs could be left square, beveled or rounded at the back, or square caps can go over the tops (Fig. 5-16J). Make the squares to overlap about ½ inch all round and bevel the exposed edges.

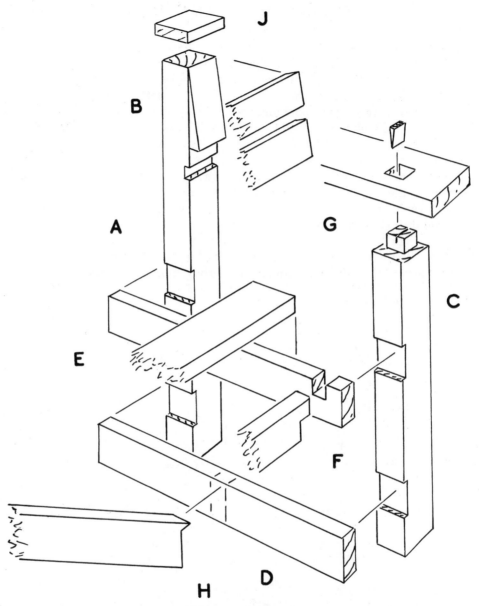

Fig. 5-16. *The relative positions of the flat strip bench parts.*

14. Check that the bench stands firmly on a level surface and is upright. You might have to take a little off one or more legs. Remove any roughness and finish the wood with paint or preservative.

DOWELED CHAIR WITH LIFT-OFF SEAT

One problem with garden furniture that is left outside is the marking of the seat, by rain, falling leaves, or fouling by animals. If the seat can be taken off and stored under cover or even left outside with its surface downward, much of the trouble is avoided. This chair has a slatted seat that can be taken off (Fig. 5-17).

This is a simple chair without arms, of the type that might be used at a table for an open-air meal. The same ideas could be used for an armchair. The parts could be joined with mortise and tenon joints, but doweled construction is shown because many workers find it easier to make strong dowel joints with the aid of a jig than to cut mortises and tenons. The chair depends for its strength on all the joints being properly bonded with waterproof glue. The parts that have dowels in their ends are mostly 1 inch thick. If they are the full thickness, the dowels could be ½ inch in diameter. If the wood was finished ⅞ of an inch thick or less, they should be ⅜ inch in diameter.

The chair's rear legs are cut from wood 3 inches thick, but that tapers to the floor and to the top to give a slope to the backrests. The seat has a slight slope for comfort, while still being suitable for sitting upright at a table.

Fig. 5-17. For a chair that is to be left outside, it is convenient to be able to remove the seat for storage or cleaning.

Materials List for Doweled Chair with Lift-Off Seat

2 rear legs	30	×	3	×	2
2 front legs	14	×	2	×	2
2 seat rails	14	×	3	×	1
2 bottom rails	14	×	2	×	1
2 crosswise rails	14	×	2	×	1
2 backrests	18	×	3	×	1
4 seat slats	20	×	3	×	1
2 seat ends	15	×	1	×	1

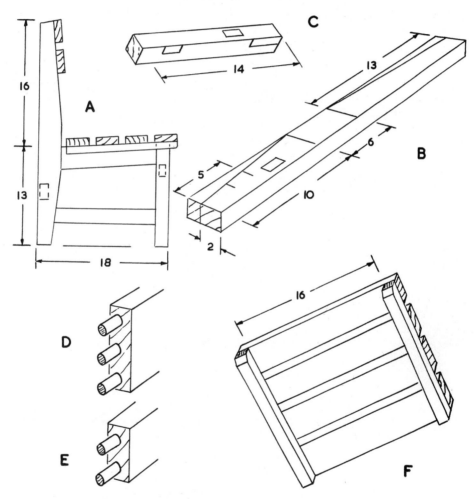

Fig. 5-18. Many parts of the chair are glued and doweled. The strips on the seat make an assembly to fit over the chair frame.

1. The side view shown in Fig. 5-18A shows the slope of the seat and overall sizes. Draw the main lines up to the seat level to get the angle that the seat support parts make.

2. Mark out the rear legs (Fig. 5-18B). There is 6 inches left parallel at seat level, and then the front edges taper from there to leave both ends 2 inches square. Mark on the edge the position of the seat rail (Fig. 5-19A) and on the side the position of the rear rail. Cut the tapers.

3. Mark and make the pair of front legs (Fig. 5-18C).

4. Make the two bottom rails 2 inches deep and the seat rails 3 inches deep (Fig. 5-19B). The angles of the ends can be found from the full-size drawing.

5. Mark out the ends of the rails and the legs they connect for dowels. It should be possible to arrange three on the 3-inch depth (Fig. 5-18D) and two on the 2-inch depth (Fig. 5-18E).

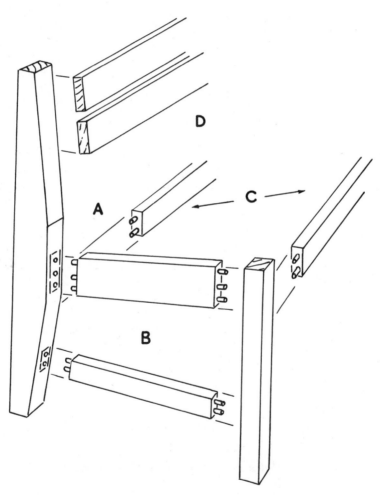

Fig. 5-19. The parts of the chair are assembled.

6. Mark and make the rails that go across the chair back and front (Fig. 5-19C). Both have square ends and two dowels. A suitable width for the chair over the legs is 16 inches.

7. The seat consists of four crosswise slats joined to pieces at the ends (Fig. 5-18F). This assembly drops over the chair frame. Get the seat sizes from the frame and make it so the end pieces press reasonably tightly over the parts that support it. The seat is unlikely to move out of place in use. There should not be any need for a fastener to keep it there. Have the tops of the seat slats well rounded and round the corners of the assembly. If everything is made exactly square and to size, the seat should fit either way. Because this is unlikely, mark on the underside of the seat which edge is to come to the front.

8. Remove any surplus glue that has squeezed out of joints and finish the chair with paint or preservative.

SAWBUCK CHAIR

A chair with legs arranged like a sawbuck or sawing trestle is novel and quite practical. The arrangement can give stability with lightness. This chair shown in Fig. 5-20 has the legs arranged asymetrically. There is an extension to the rear that prevents the chair from tipping backward and provides attachments for the backrest supports. The sizes given will make a chair of moderate size, but the same method could be used for a larger chair or extended in length to make a two-seat bench.

All of the wood suggested is 3-inch-×-1-inch section and this could be hard or softwood. If the chair is expected to be pulled about on a stone or concrete surface, a hardwood will be better able *to resist the grain of the feet being torn and splintered.* This would also be stronger at the halving joint in the legs. If softwood is used or you have doubts about the strength of the joint you cut, there can be a cover piece screwed on inside the crossing where it will not show. The parts should be glued, but the main parts are bolted and the others screwed.

1. Setting out the shape is not as complicated as it might first appear. The general shape is shown in Fig. 5-21A, but the first step is to set out using centerlines (Fig. 5-21B). Draw a floor line, and another representing the centerline of the seat support parallel to it (Fig. 5-21C), with a square line at what will be the front of the chair. Go 24 inches along the floor line from this and join that point to the top of the square line (Fig. 5-21D). Draw the other diagonal from

Materials List for Sawbuck Chair			
2 legs	24	× 3	× 1
2 legs	28	× 3	× 1
2 backrest			
supports	30	× 3	× 1
2 backrests	18	× 3	× 1
2 seat supports	20	× 3	× 1
4 seat slats	18	× 3	× 1
1 bottom rail	14	× 3	× 1

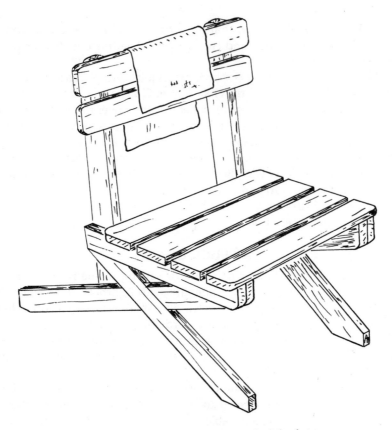

Fig. 5-20. A sawbuck chair gets its stability from the spread of the feet.

17 inches along the top line (Fig. 5-21E). Go 9 inches up the rear leg line and draw the backrest support through it (Fig. 5-21F). If you measure 1½ inches each side of these centerlines, you will get the wood widths and you can finish off the drawing as in Fig. 5-21A. This completed drawing is necessary to get the shapes to cut most of the parts.

2. Make the two sets of legs from this drawing and cut halving joints between them (Fig. 5-22A).

3. Note how the parts will be put together on the front view (Fig. 5-21G). The seat supports are outside, the crossed legs come next, and the backrest supports are inside.

4. Make the seat supports (Figs. 5-21H and 5-22B). Leave some excess length at the rear for trimming off after the other parts are joined to it.

5. Make the two backrest supports (Figs. 5-21J and 5-22C). They will bolt at the marked positions to the legs and seat supports. Drill the holes and make a trail assembly. At the front of the seat, its support is screwed to the legs. If the trial is satisfactory, glue the joints and secure them permanently.

6. Make a bottom rail to screw to the backrest supports inside the legs (Fig. 5-21K). Prepare the backrest pieces (Fig. 5-22D). They overlap the supports and

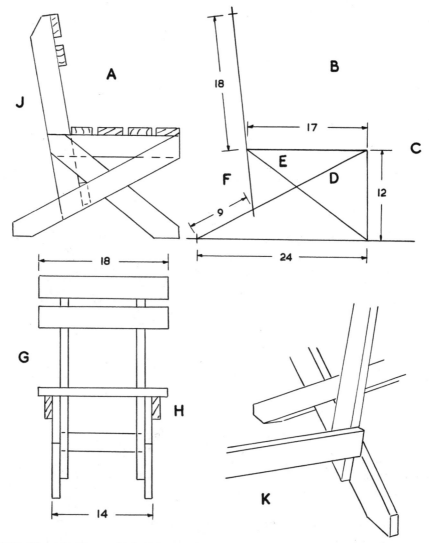

Fig. 5-21. The end of the sawbuck chair must be set out to get the legs in the correct position, with the back supports overlapping the legs.

should have rounded corners as well as rounded front edges. Glue and screw on these strips and the bottom rail. Check that the assembly stands upright.

7. Make the seat slats. Round their top edges and round the corners of the outside ones. Glue and screw them on, with the front one level at the front of the supports and the others evenly spaced.

8. This completes assembly and the chair can be finished with paint, varnish, or preservative.

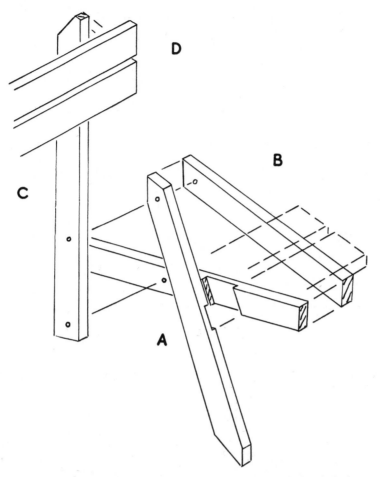

D

B

C

A

Fig. 5-22. The legs are halved, but other parts overlap and are screwed or bolted.

TUSK TENON SEAT

Construction where parts have tenons extending through to be held by wedges is particularly appropriate for garden furniture. That type of joint is suited to the fairly heavy boards of much exterior construction. There are at least two structural advantages. If wood shrinks, you can pull joints tight by hammering the wedges further in, and if the article is completely assembled with tusk tenon joints it can be disassembled if you want to pack it away for the winter. The method is not very suitable for light assemblies, but if you are using fairly thick wood it is a good structural technique and furniture made that way will give a novel appearance to the amenities of your garden or yard.

Use hardwood at least 1½ inches thick; it need not be planed. Slabs cut across a log are particularly appropriate. Some parts have to be wide and you will need to find pieces of sufficient width. Boards can be joined, and some methods of making up width for exterior parts are described in Chapter 2.

Materials List for Tusk Tenon Seat

2 ends	35	×	21	×	1¾
2 arms	22	×	4	×	1¾
2 caps	7	×	4	×	1¾
wedges from	50	×	2	×	1¾
For chair:					
1 back	36	×	10	×	1¾
2 seats	36	×	9	×	1¾
For bench:					
1 back	60	×	10	×	1¾
2 seats	60	×	9	×	1¾
1 rail	60	×	5	×	1¾

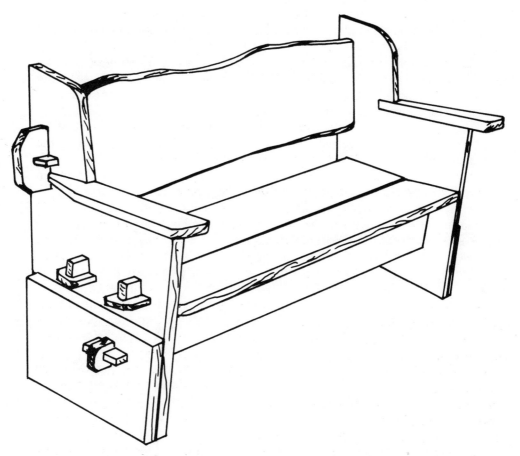

Fig. 5-23. Tusk tenons form a good way to join lengthwise parts to the end of a bench.

The wood could be used with waney edges to give an interesting effect (Fig. 5-23) or the boards could be finished with parallel edges for a more formal design. Construction is the same, in any case, except that with waney edges on both sides you should work from a centerline when squaring and marking joints. You cannot work from an edge; that is possible only if one or more sides are straight.

This design could be made as a single seat or extended to make a bench. A single seat might be about 24 inches wide. That would be rigid enough without a bottom rail, but if it is lengthened to 48 inches or more the extra stiffness of a rail would be advisable. As shown the tusks and wedges are plain. If the seat is to be given a formal finish for use on a patio or elsewhere near the house and a less rural appearance is preferred, they could be decorated with shaped ends.

1. The key shapes are the two ends (Fig. 5-24A). Set out the shape to suit the wood available, including end views of the lengthwise parts. Allow for mortises slightly more than half the width of the boards. If a seat board is 9 inches wide, a mortise 5 inches wide will be about right. Exact size is not crucial. Include the bottom rail position if it is a bench you are making, but omit it for a chair. The seat is given a slight hallow; a drop of 1 inch in a total width of 18 inches is suggested.

2. Prepare the wood for the lengthwise parts. The important measurements are the distances between shoulders each side of the tenons. The back, seat, and rail should be marked out together (Fig. 5-24B) with at least 6 inches of extra wood for the tenons extending at the ends.

3. Mark the tenon widths and the matching widths of the mortises. Cut the sides of the tenons, but do not trim them to length. Most of the waste in the mortises can be removed by drilling, but they should be trimmed to shape with a chisel. Each tenon should slide easily through its mortise. Excessive play can be avoided, but that would be better than fitting the parts for a drive fit.

4. It is advisable to adopt a standard size of wedge (Fig. 5-24C). Then it will not matter where you use them if you have to reassemble. The slot in each tenon must allow the wedge to slot in easily, but its inner edge must come within the mortised part (Fig. 5-24D). When you drive the wedge in, it forces the tenon outward by its bearing against the surface of the mortised piece and there is no risk of it touching the bottom of the slot (which would prevent further tightening).

5. Make a trial assembly. If that is satisfactory, trim and bevel the ends of the tenons (Figs. 5-24E and 5-25A). Do not cut them back too far because the wedges will tighten against end grain, and that could break out if the end is too narrow.

6. Complete the shaping of the ends. Hollow the bottoms (Fig. 5-25B) so that bearing only at the sides will reduce the risk of rocking on uneven ground. The top above the seat back can be rounded, but a capping nailed or screwed on (Fig. 5-25C) would match the arms and prevent rainwater from entering the grain.

7. The arms (Figs. 5-24F and 5-25D) could be parallel pieces, but they are shown with some shaping. Have straight inner edges over the seat end and a curved front end, with the outside shaped back to overlap with a notch. Screw

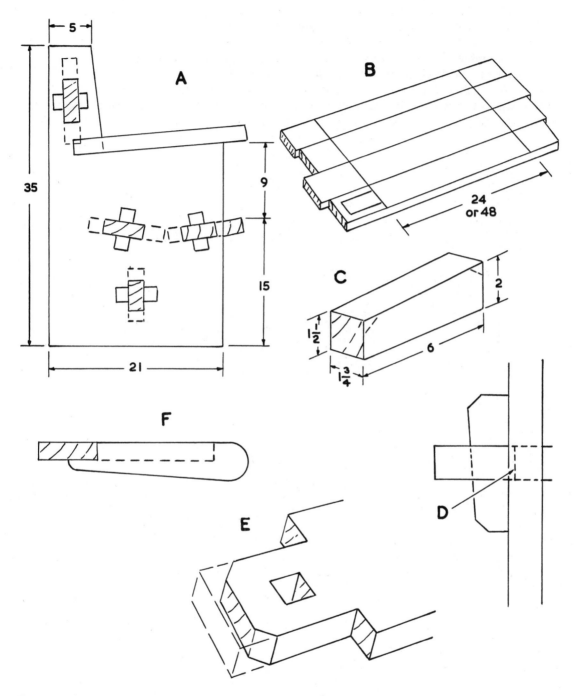

Fig. 5-24. *If natural wood is used for a bench, sizes will have to be adapted to suit.*

down into the seat end, preferably with counterbored and plugged holes, or you could glue in dowels instead of screwing.

8. Assemble all parts and drive the wedges fairly tight. Usually, after exposure for a few weeks, you will be able to tighten them further. If the wood has a sawn finish and it is not a hardwood with its own resistance to exposure, treat it with preservative. If you have used planed boards, they could have a painted finish.

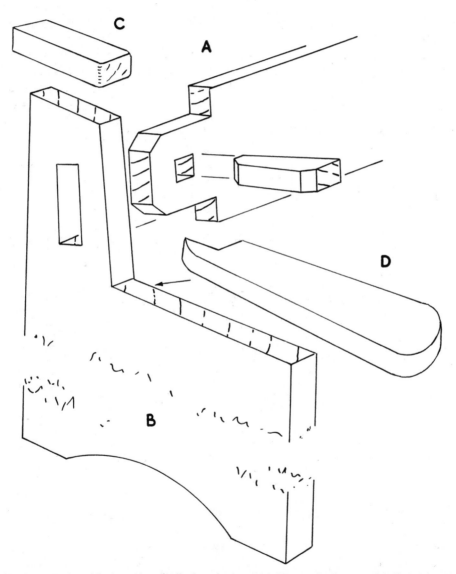

Fig. 5-25. *Each end has mortises for the lengthwise parts. Tenons are large and pulled tight with wedges.*

PARK BENCH

Although much garden seating is crude and simple compared with chairs used indoors, there is a place for better made furniture. In a formal garden or on a well-equipped deck or patio, something that is not of a very high standard of construction will be rather obvious and not suited to its surroundings. Sometimes a seat is made to commemorate some event. It could be a special anniversary, a particular happening, or even the moving to a new address. Somewhere on the seat would be carved, painted, or a plaque added giving details. In that case the seat should be worthy of its importance.

A seat for an important situation should be made of good wood, with cut joints rather than screws or nails, and the total effect should be pleasing and functional. Seats of this type are often seen in public parks and gardens. There is a similarity about their designs due to comfort and appearance requirements having to be met. The seat shown in Fig. 5-26 is a basic form and possible variations are described. The material should be seasoned hardwood planed all round and free from large knots, particularly in the lengthwise parts. An overall length of

Fig. 5-26. A formal bench with parts made from planed wood can make a comfortable resting place in a garden.

Materials List for Park Bench

2 rear legs	36	× 4	×	2
2 front legs	25	× 2	×	2
2 seat rails	19	× 3	×	1
2 bottom rails	19	× 2	×	1
2 arms	22	× 4	×	1
4 seat pieces	60	× 3	×	1
1 front seat rail	60	× 4	×	1
1 rear seat rail	60	× 3	×	1
2 seat supports	19	× 3	×	1
1 back top rail	60	× 5	×	1
or	60	× 3	×	1
1 back bottom rail	60	× 3	×	1
11 back slats	14	× 2	×	⅝
or				
1 back slat	14	× 6	×	⅝
2 back slats	14	× 5	×	⅝
2 back slats	14	× 4	×	⅝
2 back slats	14	× 3	×	⅝

60 inches will accommodate three sitters, but other lengths are possible—down to a single seat. Two single seats might commemorate a wedding anniversary or other double occasion, but there is more wood and work than required for making a two-person bench. On the other hand, independent chairs allow you to locate them throughout the yard or garden.

The bench has a hollowed seat and a tilted back that is decorated with vertical slats. Except for the bend in the rear legs, shaping of the arms and possible shaping of the top back rail, nearly all the parts are straight. The wood may be machine-planed, but on the visible surfaces the plane marks should be removed by sanding or hand planing if the bench is to be given a clear or untreated finish.

1. A full-size layout of the end view will be useful, but it is not essential because most information is shown on the drawing. The back legs and seat supports can be laid out on the wood (Fig. 5-27A). Notice the positions of rails and other lengthwise parts in relation to the ends (Fig. 5-27B).

2. Mark out the rear legs (Fig. 5-28A). The bend comes above the seat level. Do not make this a sharp angle; curve between the straight sections, particularly toward the rear. Mark on the positions of all joints so that this leg layout can be used as a guide when marking other parts. Cut the legs to shape, but leave some excess length, at both ends, to be trimmed off after joints have been cut.

3. Mark out the front legs (Fig. 5-28B) with joint positions matching those on the rear legs. The front seat rail will have its upper edge level with the tops of the seat pieces (Figs. 5-27C and 5-28C). Measure the actual wood being used for the seat to get the height of the top of the rail. At the tops of the legs, mark where the underside of the arm will come and leave more than enough above that for making and cutting the tenons later.

4. The bottom end rail (Fig. 5-28D) is a simple piece with tenons at its ends and a mortise position slightly forward of halfway for a lengthwise rail (Fig. 5-29A).

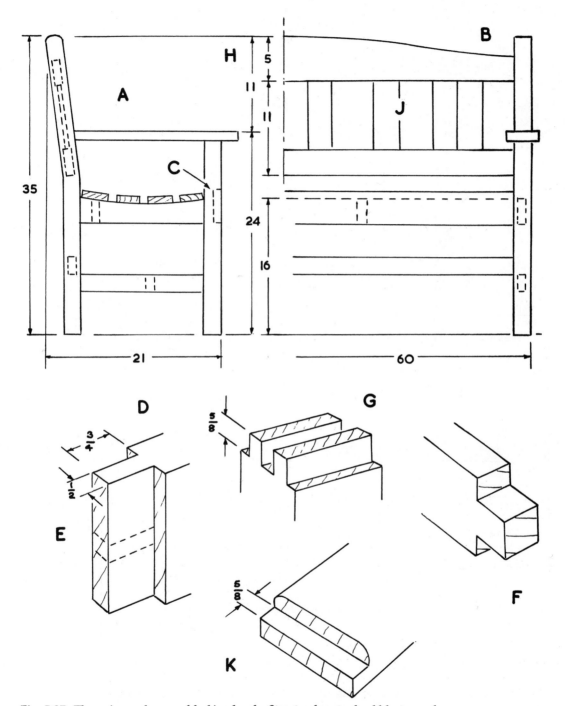

Fig. 5-27. These sizes make a good-looking bench. Structural parts should be tenoned.

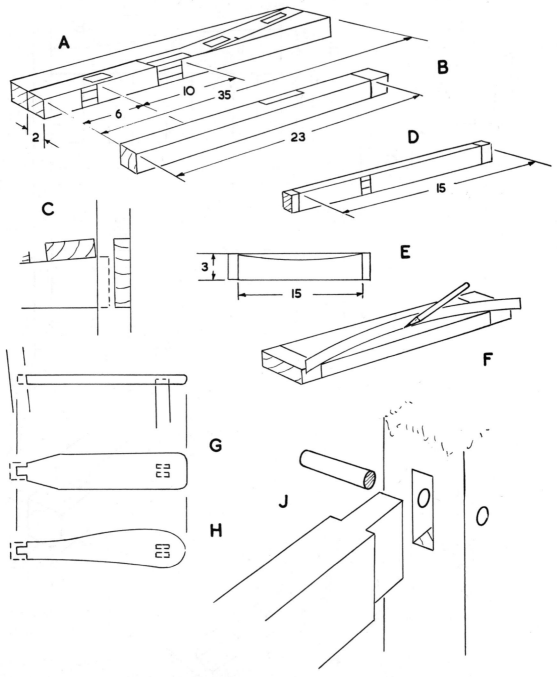

Fig. 5-28. Make the individual parts first. Mark and cut tenoned joints so they can be pegged.

5. Make the seat rails the same length between shoulders as the bottom rails. The amount of hallow in the top is not crucial, but a drop of ¾ of an inch at the center will be satisfactory (Figs. 5-28E and 5-29B). This can be drawn by penciling around a sprung lath (Fig. 5-28F). A rear rail (Fig. 5-29C) goes under the back seat piece and will have two seat supports (Fig. 5-29D) evenly spaced and attached to it and the front seat rail. Mark the curves on these now, so all parts have matching shapes, but do not cut them to length yet.

6. Make the pair of arms. They could be simple, mainly parallel, pieces (Fig. 5-28G) or have shaped outlines (Fig. 5-28H). In any case, well round the top and front edges. Leave more than enough for cutting the tenons at the back and mark where the front legs will join.

7. All of the end parts can be joined with stub tenons. It should be sufficient for them to enter mortises about ¾ of an inch, with a tenon thickness of ½ of an inch on wood of the sizes specified in Fig. 5-27D. The parts of 2 inch or less depth can have the tenons as cut, but for 3-inch pieces the tenons could be divided (Fig. 5-27E) if you prefer. Where the rear seat and bottom rails join, allow for narrower tenons going right through (Fig. 5-27F).

8. At the arms, the tenon into the rear legs will be the same as elsewhere, except the shoulders should slope to match the leg angle. At the front legs, the tenons cannot penetrate very far into the arms and it is better to make them double (Fig. 5-27G) to give a greater glue area.

9. Assemble the ends now and cut mortises for the lengthwise parts later, but it is easier to cut joints in separate pieces of wood. Determine the sizes of lengthwise parts and cut mortises in the legs and end rails now even if you do not make the matching tenons yet.

10. Assemble the pair of ends. Use clamps to draw the joints tight. Check squareness and that the opposite ends match and are without twist. Extra security of joints can be given by drilling for dowels across them; one ¼-inch dowel in each joint should be sufficient (Fig. 5-28J).

11. Mark out the front seat rail (Fig. 5-29E) and use it as a guide to lengths between shoulders when making other lengthwise parts. Mark on it the positions of seat supports and round its top edges. On a 60-inch length, two evenly spaced supports will be enough. Allow for the supports having narrow tenons right through or stub tenons if you do not want end grain to show at the front.

12. Make the rear seat rail (Fig. 5-29F). This will be slightly longer than the front seat rail as it goes between end rails and not legs. Mark the bottom rail (Fig. 5-29G); it will be the same length. Both have narrow tenons at the ends.

13. Mark the positions of the seat supports on the two long rails. Cut these to fit and glue the joints. Check squareness, as the accuracy of this assembly affects squareness of the complete bench.

14. The bottom rail between the rear legs is a simple piece (Fig. 5-29H) that is the same length between shoulders as the front seat rail.

15. The two back rails should also be this length. Figure 5-26 shows two parallel pieces, but if you want to carve, paint, or attach a plaque to the bench the center of the top rail is the place for this commemoration. The top rail is drawn with a curved top to provide this space (Fig. 5-27H). The ends are the same depth

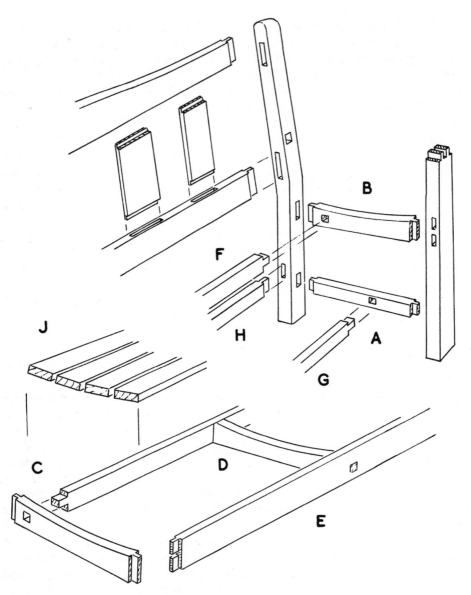

Fig. 5-29. *All parts except the seat slats are tenoned.*

as straight rails would be. Therefore, the joints to the rear legs are the same. Make the two back rails to the shape you want. Ends are tenoned to suit the mortises in the legs.

16. The back could have a pattern of similar parallel upright slats (as shown in Fig. 5-26). If the top rail is curved up at the center, this could be complemented by having a wide center slat, and then reducing the widths of the others toward the ends (Fig. 5-27J). This would provide enough space on the center one for an inscription in place of, or in addition to, any on the top rail.

17. As the slats are not very thick, they can have barefaced tenons on their ends (Fig. 5-27K). The front edges can be rounded. Make the slats and cut the joints. Assemble the slats to the rails while again checking squareness that will affect the finished bench.

18. All the lengthwise parts can now be joined to the ends. The seat and back assemblies should pull the bench square. Have it standing on a flat surface so that there is no risk of twist. Draw the joints tight and put dowels across most of them.

19. The seat pieces (Fig. 5-29J) should have their upper edges rounded and their ends extending a short distance over the end rails (where they can also be rounded). Mark where the crossings come and drill for two screws in each piece at each place. Brass screws could finish on the surface or you can counterbore and plug them.

20. The bench could be finished by painting, but if a good hardwood has been used it would look better if the grain is visible. If it is a durable wood that will withstand exposure unprotected, it could be left to weather to a natural shade. Otherwise, a clear varnish could be used. This does not have to be a high gloss, but several coats of semiglossy varnish can be more effective. Marine varnish will have the longest life.

SWINGING SEAT

A swinging seat or glider for two people makes a pleasant place to relax. It can be hung from a porch or it could have its own supports for use anywhere in the garden or yard. There are several ways of making such a seat and many sizes are possible. The seat shown in Fig. 5-30 is shaped to provide comfort as it is, but it could be improved with cushions. The size is intended to suit two persons with plenty of space. A bigger seat could be made in the same way, but if it is made much longer the sections of the lengthwise wood should be increased.

The ropes or chains attach to a strip that goes the length of the back and to reinforced front uprights. Details of a support follow. That needs to be fairly high to give a more comfortable swinging action than could be possible with short ropes.

All the parts can be made of softwood, but a durable hardwood, such as oak, would be better suited to exposure. If the suggested canopy is made, it will protect the wood from severe weather as well as shield the users from sunlight and showers.

Materials List for Swinging Seat						
2 seat rails	30	×	6	×	1½
2 uprights	27	×	4	×	1½
2 support blocks	4	×	4	×	1½
2 arms	33	×	4	×	1½
1 hanging strip	72	×	4	×	1½
1 bottom strip	60	×	4	×	2
7 seat slats	64	×	2	×	1½
4 back slats	64	×	2	×	1½

Fig. 5-30. A swinging seat can hang in a porch or be supported by a frame.

1. The key assembly that settles the sizes of many other parts is the end (Fig. 5-31A). Draw this full size. How much slope to give the uprights is not crucial, but about 10 degrees is suitable. The curve of the seat can be drawn freehand. Let it dip about 1 inch from the top of the wood and curve down to vertical at the front (Fig. 5-31B). Allow for the 2-inch seat slats being spaced about 1½ inches apart. Use a similar spacing at the back; it can be taken to a different height if you prefer. Curve the tops of the uprights (Fig. 5-31C).

2. Make the end parts and check that the opposite assemblies will be a matching pair. Although it would be possible to merely lap the parts and glue and screw them, notches help in locating the joints and preventing later movement. Keep the notches in the uprights quite shallow (Fig. 5-31D); ¼ inch will be enough. Where the back hanging strip fits, the shallow notch will be in that and enough must be cut from the rear upright for the rear faces to come level (Fig. 5-31E).

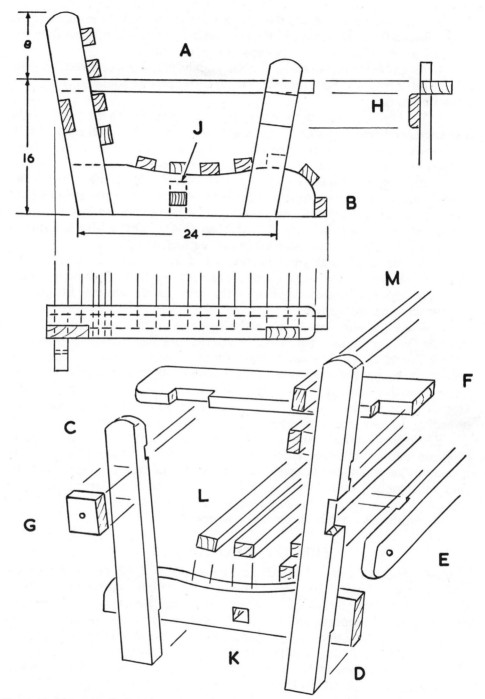

Fig. 5-31. *The seat is built as a unit, with strong parts where the hanging chains come.*

3. Make the arms to fit into the uprights and come level at the outside (Fig. 5-31F). Round the front corners of the arms and round all edges that will be exposed. Take the sharpness off the tops of the uprights.

4. Assemble the pair of ends. The arms can be glued and screwed. The seat rails are better held with bolts through. Two ½-inch-diameter bolts at each crossing should be sufficient.

5. The front ropes attach to an eyebolt, in each end, where the front upright is strengthened with a block outside (Fig. 5-31G) below arm level (Fig. 5-31H). Its exposed edges can be rounded. The eyebolt should go through with large washers at each side of the wood to spread the pressure.

6. Although the seat and back slats provide considerable stiffness lengthwise, strength in that direction is mainly provided by the back hanging strip and another underneath between the seat rails (Fig. 5-31J). The one underneath should be tenoned into the seat rails (Fig. 5-31K). Make this before the other lengthwise parts and use it to hold the ends while getting their lengths.

7. Let the back hanging rail extend up to 6 inches beyond the seat ends. Drill the extension for the hanging ropes or shackles for chains. Round the ends. Assemble these two lengthwise pieces to the ends. Check that they fit squarely and the ends will be upright.

8. Make the seat slats to fit on the seat rails, either level with them or extending a short distance (Fig. 5-31L). Make the back slats in a similar way (Fig. 5-31M). Round all the slats' outer edges before screwing them into place. It is helpful to use a piece of scrap wood of the correct width to keep regular spacings. Uneven spacing can appear very obvious when the seat is unoccupied. An extended seat might require an intermediate support for the seat slats, but providing they are strong enough, slight springiness is an advantage.

9. Modern synthetic rope is very strong and most of it will stand up to exposure without suffering. Therefore the seat could be hung with rope about ½ inch diameter (knotted or spliced at the ends). Alternatively, there could be chains that would require shackles to the eyebolts and either large shackles or eyebolts through the rear hanging strip for smaller shackles.

10. Finish the wood with paint or preservative.

SWINGING SEAT SUPPORT

If the swinging seat is to be located in the garden or yard, either in a permanent position or as a freestanding structure, there has to be a support that is high enough to allow a gentle swinging action, wide enough for the seat to move without touching the supports, and with a sufficient base to keep the assembly free from tipping. If the support is to be moveable, the base should be wide enough back to front to resist tipping with the most energetic swinging. That means feet should be about as long as the support is high. If the base is to be bolted or staked down, it need not project much more than the spread of the legs.

The support is for a seat, as just described, and is basically as shown in Fig. 5-30. The height suits the seat, and its length should be sufficient to have the legs about 24 inches further apart than the overall length of the seat. As with

Materials List for Swinging Seat Support

2 legs	102	×	4	×	2
2 feet	96	×	4	×	2
2 rails	48	×	4	×	2
1 beam	108	×	6	×	2
4 gussets	12	×	6	×	1
1 stiffener	100	×	4	×	2

4 steel brackets with 6 inch legs

the seat, the support could be made of softwood protected with preservative, but it would be better made of a durable hardwood. Details that follow are for a support without a canopy. If a canopy is to be fitted now or later, there are some slight modifications that should be allowed for during construction. See the following project.

1. Set out the main lines of an end view (Fig. 5-32A) to get the lengths of the legs and the angles to cut the parts. A half view at one side of the centerline will tell you all you need.

2. The wood for the beam and the legs should be chosen for straightness of grain and the absence of flaws. The beam (Fig. 5-32B) is a plain piece, extending far enough to cover the brackets.

3. At the tops, cut the legs to fit around the beam and against each other (Fig. 5-32C). Mark where the rail and foot come on each piece, but the bottom need not be cut until the foot is attached (Fig. 5-32D).

4. Prepare the feet (Fig. 5-32E) and mark where their legs come. Bevel the ends.

5. Bring the top of each pair of legs together and join them with gussets, cut with their grain running across (Fig. 5-32F). Arrange the width of the slot so that it will be a tight fit on the beam. Glue and screw the gussets (although there could also be bolts through) clear of where the brackets will come.

6. Bolt the legs to the feet and the rails to the legs. Cut off any surplus wood and take off any sharp edges or corners.

7. Add the beam and the bottom stiffener with the legs on edge. Screw and bolt the beam between the tops of the legs and use steel brackets underneath to provide stiffness (Fig. 5-32G). When you fit the stiffener to the feet, compare distances at tops and bottoms of the legs and check squareness by measuring diagonals. A bolt through each foot will be better than screws.

8. Bring the assembly upright and check stability and squareness.

9. The seat ropes could be taken around the beam, possibly located with small blocks of wood to act as cleats (Fig. 5-32H) to prevent the turns sliding along. If chain is used, there should be eyebolts through the beam (Fig. 5-32J) to take shackles. Locate them to suit the width of the seat. If they are wider apart, they will help to restrict lengthwise movement of the seat.

10. Finish the wood with paint or preservative.

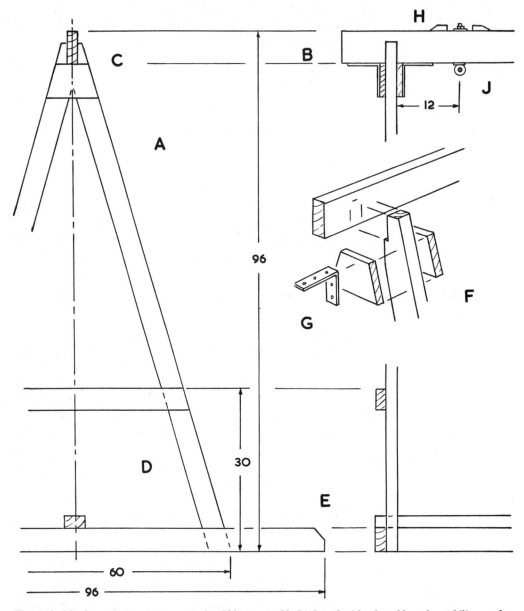

Fig. 5-32. The frame for a swinging seat should be reasonably high and with a broad base for stability and a satisfactory action.

CANOPY FOR SWINGING SEAT

A roof over the swinging seat and its support (Figs. 5-31 and 5-32) will make an attractive unit that should look good in any garden or yard situation. The roof can take the form of a canopy large enough to shield from overhead sunlight, as well as protect both the users and the woodwork from rain. Size can be adjusted

Materials List for Canopy for Swinging Seat

2 ends	72	×	6	×	1
2 eaves	108	×	2	×	2
4 strips	112	×	2	×	1

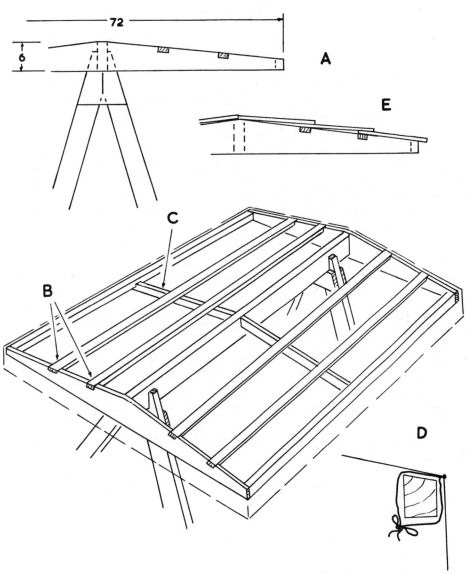

Fig. 5-33. The support for a canopy can be mounted on the top of the frame supporting a swinging seat.

to suit your needs. If the canopy is to be made longer, the beam length should be increased when making the support. As shown in Fig. 5-33, the canopy size suits the support as suggested in the previous project.

The basic framework can be covered in several ways. It can have a canvas top that is tied on and can be removed and stored under cover when not required. There could be plywood sheets permanently attached. An attractive finish could be achieved by using shingles. If they are to be used, their sizes will have to be checked and the lengthwise strips spaced to suit.

The framework should be kept light. As it is to be covered, softwood should be sufficiently durable. The suggested size has the ends the same depth as the beam, but if you make it much wider the ends should be deepened to give sufficient slope to the top.

1. Mark out and cut the two ends (Fig. 5-33A). At the eaves, the 2-inch-square strip goes between the ends and will be screwed there. At the other strips, cut notches for them to let in (Fig. 5-33B). Space the strips evenly for canvas or plywood covering, but arrange more, if required, to suit shingles.

2. Make the eaves strips the same length as the beam. Screw the ends to the beam and to the strips. Check that the pieces are horizontal in all directions. Stand back and see that the assembly looks right in relation to the beam and other parts. Check squareness as from above.

3. Put the two intermediate support pieces in (Fig. 5-33C) and add the lengthwise strips to complete the assembly.

4. If the top is to be covered with plywood, that should be exterior grade. Along the ridge put a cover strip to reduce the risk of water entering the edges of the veneers. Cover any joints with similar strips.

5. A canvas cover could be made with proofed canvas or with plastic-coated fabric, arranged with a hanging border that goes below the wood and is held on with tapes or cords around the eaves and other parts (Fig. 5-33D). If you prefer, this could be finished with a fringe. An overall green color would be appropriate if you do not want to attract attention to the seat. You could give it a bright effect with red and white stripes or other vivid colors.

6. With shingles, start at the eaves and nail (Fig. 5-33E). Support underneath with another hammer or an iron block as you progress along the strips. Along the ridge, use a cover strip or two shingles cut at angles and cemented.

7. Finish the wood appropriately to match other parts.

6
CHAPTER

Tables

After chairs, tables are most in demand for outdoor use. There are many manufactured tables, some of which can be folded, and everyone is familiar with the picnic table with benches attached. There are several other tables that can be made for permanent outdoor use or to carry in and out as required. Many tables have similar construction to chairs so that they make matching sets. Some rustic tables are described in Chapter 4, but in a more formal garden—where chairs of the type described in Chapter 5 are used—the tables should mostly be of similar type with jointed construction and a good finish.

The notes at the beginning of Chapter 5 concerning materials and techniques are also applicable to the making of tables.

The main requirement of a table, whatever its design or construction, is a top that is level and held rigidly in place for normal use. The structure underneath is there to achieve this end and it fails in its purpose if the top slopes, is uneven, or is liable to fall over. This requirement should be borne in mind when planning and making a table. If a table is to remain outside in all weather, the top will usually have to be made of solid boards. Even the best marine or exterior grades of plywood are liable to suffer if left exposed for long periods, but plywood will make effective tops for tables that are stored under cover. Most other manufactured boards suffer from the same problems as plywood when exposed to prolonged sunlight, rain, or frost conditions. The availability of suitable materials for the top could be the governing factor in deciding on the table you will make.

Table sizes should be related to seats. With chair seats about 15 inches from the ground, the tabletop should be 27 inches to 30 inches high. For most people, slightly less is better rather than slightly higher. If the table is only to be for drinks and magazines near a lounging chair, it can be lower—possibly down to 24 inches. If you make it much lower, someone will mistake it for a seat (so make it strong enough to sit on). Any table intended to be used for meals should have its top 12 inches to 15 inches above the chair or bench seat level. Anyone standing can use a table 30 inches high. If the table you make is not intended for anyone in a normal chair, it could be 3 inches or so higher.

A table needs a fairly broad base to stand steadily. In general, avoid making a table that is higher than its width and length. You might have to reduce one way in some cases. That means a tabletop should be at least 27 inches one or both ways. You can increase stability by letting the bottoms of the legs project outside of the top, but extensions of more than an inch or so will be a nuisance.

Tabletops should be stiff enough to avoid warping, but that does not mean they should be thick if there is adequate framing. They need not be solid. Gaps between boards allow rain to run through. Light slats can be arranged with spaces to make a light top for a portable table. Obviously gaps should not be very wide. Even with a cloth over, anything wider than about ½ inch could cause some items to tip or small ones to fall through.

STRIP TABLE

Figure 6-1 shows a light rigid table that is easy for two persons to carry about. If made of suitable wood, it could be left outside, but it is the type of table that could also have uses in a greenhouse, playroom, or other indoor situation when it is not needed outside. The size suggested makes the table suitable for outdoor meals with many of the chairs described in Chapter 5.

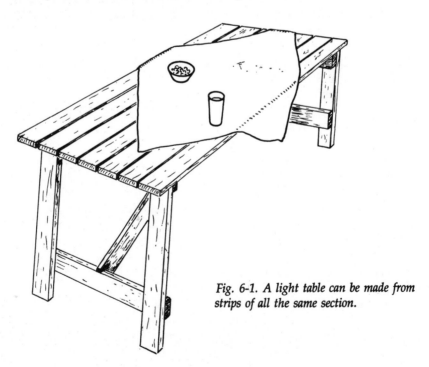

Fig. 6-1. A light table can be made from strips of all the same section.

Materials List for Strip Table

4 legs	27 × 3 × 1		
4 rails	24 × 3 × 1		
1 cleat	26 × 3 × 1		
1 rail	42 × 3 × 1		
2 struts	36 × 3 × 1		
7 top strips	48 × 3 × 1		

The design is based on strips of wood of all the same sections. In the example, the wood is 3 inches wide and 1 inch thick, but the sizes could be adapted to suit wood of other sizes. For this method of construction, it is important that the top has an odd number of strips in it so that there is a central one over the lengthwise rail. The overall width suggested suits seven 3-inch pieces with narrow gaps between. If you are using other width strips, experiment with them to arrive at a suitable width top before planning the other sizes.

All of the parts are glued and screwed. There is insufficient thickness for screws to be counterbored, so use brass or other damp-resisting screws and choose lengths that will go almost through the second piece.

1. Make the two end trestles (Fig. 6-2A and B), using glue and four screws at each crossing. Check squareness and that opposite ends match.

2. Notch the top bars of the trestles to take the rail (Fig. 6-2C).

3. Make the rail 6 inches less than the top is to be to allow overhang at the ends. Notch the ends to fit the trestle (Fig. 6-2D) and cut a notch at the center for a cleat that will go across under the top (Fig. 6-2E). Make that cleat to a length that will come to the outside edges of the top (or almost so). Bevel the undersides of its ends.

4. Prepare the top strips. Lightly round the top edges and round the ends, which will overhang the trestles by about 3 inches. Drill for two screws in each piece into the tops of the trestles. Use the rail as a guide to lengthwise spacing. Also drill the central strip for screws at about 9-inch intervals into the rail. Allow for the outside strips overhanging the trestle tops by 1 inch.

5. Glue and screw the central rail into the notches in the trestles. Put the cleat across in its notch and screw it there. Over this glue and screw the central top strip. Add the outer strips while checking that the assembly is square as you do this.

6. Position the other top strips evenly between those already attached.

7. Invert the table and drive screws upward through the cleat into each top strip.

8. Although the two diagonal struts come near the center of the table, their ends can be marked by having the table on its side. This way strips can be put across the edge and the contact places can be outlined. Allow for the bottom notch overlapping the depth of the trestle rail by about 2 inches. The overhang at the top bears on its edge and the surplus is cut off (Fig. 6-2F). At the top of a strut,

allow it to go about 5 inches past the center of the table, and then cut its edge parallel with the top (Fig. 6-2G).

9. The struts are positioned on opposite sides of the central rail. Screw them first to the trestle rails. You can then move their tops a little along the central rail until, before screwing to it, you have checked that the legs are square to the top.

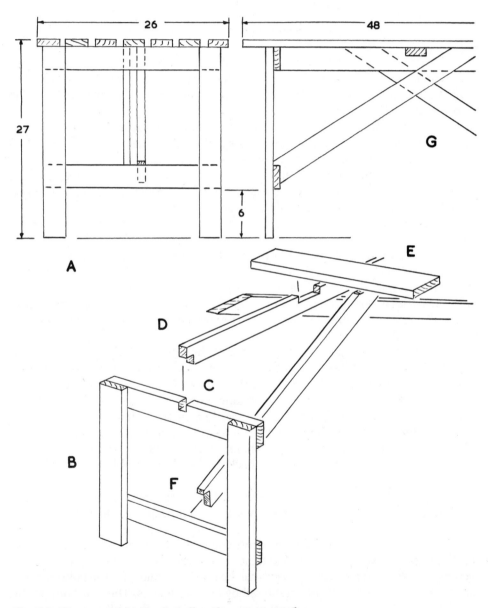

Fig. 6-2. *The suggested table sizes allow the parts to overlap.*

10. That completes construction and the table can be left untreated if it is a weather-resisting hardwood. If it is softwood it should be painted. Hardwood can be painted or varnished. In either case, the wood could be treated with preservative. If the table is to be used for eating from, it should be left some time before placing food on it.

SPLAYED-LEGS TABLE

If table legs slope outward both ways, the appearance is improved and there is an advantage in stability. The outline covered by the feet can be at or outside the lines of the top. With vertical legs, this could only be arranged by having the legs joining the top at its corners (which is ugly and inconvenient).

Anyone interested in geometry will know that there is a problem if the legs splay much. The actual section of the legs will no longer be square, but will take on a diamond shape. This complicate the preparation of wood and the cutting of joints. If the splay is kept slight, however, any errors are also slight and can be taken care of in the practicalities of construction. Shapes and fits of parts should be close enough not to be noticed.

The table shown in Fig. 6-3 has its legs sloping out to cover the same area on the ground as the top; it should stand firmly. It is shown as a small general-purpose size, but the techniques could be used to make a table of any other size.

Fig. 6-3. A table with legs splayed both ways is very stable.

Materials List for Splayed-Legs Table

4 legs	27	× 2	× 2	
2 top rails	30	× 4	× 1	
2 top rails	21	× 4	× 1	
2 bottom rails	25	× 2	× 1	
1 bottom rail	28	× 2	× 1	
4 tops	36	× 7	× 1	

The top is drawn as made up of four 7-inch-wide boards. It could be framed plywood or particleboard if the table is to be kept under cover when out of use. Decide on the size of the top before making other parts.

Almost any wood could be used. A heavy hardwood might be most suitable if the table is to be rarely moved. Softwood would make it light for portability, but a softwood top on a hardwood frame would be strong and of moderate weight.

1. Although in precision construction the leg lengths would have to be developed geometrically, differences here are so slight that you can make the end frames as if there was no compound slope. Set out the end (Fig. 6-4A) with its main lines symmetrical about a centerline (Fig. 6-4B). This can be used as a guide to the slopes of joints the other way.

2. Mark the legs, using an adjustable bevel instead of a square, but do not cut off the ends yet. Mark the top rails (Fig. 6-4C); allow about ¾ of an inch at each end for tenons. Mark the bottom rails in a similar way (Fig. 6-4D). Although there are slopes on the wider faces, lines in the other direction can be square across.

3. Make the mortise and tenon joints (Fig. 6-4E and F). Alternatively, cut the wood at the shoulders and use dowels (Fig. 6-5A and B).

4. In the other direction, mark and cut similar joints for the lengthwise top rails (Fig. 6-4G). With tenons, you can drill across and put dowels through for added strength, or you can use nails or screws from inside (Fig. 6-5C).

5. The bottom central rail (Fig. 6-4H) has tenons through the bottom and rails. Tenons here are preferable to dowels because they will have a better resistance to pulling apart under load.

6. The top can be screwed from above. If you want to attach the top without screw heads or plugs showing on top, there are two possible ways of screwing from below. If you are to use either of them it is easier to prepare the rails before assembly than to do it after assembling the framework. Individual screws can be driven as "pocket" screws in hollows gouged out (Fig. 6-5D) or made by drilling (Fig. 6-5E). Another way uses "buttons." They screw to the top, but engage with plowed grooves inside the rails (Fig. 6-5F). Buttons allow for the top expanding and contracting without the risk of splits developing.

7. Prepare the rails for either method, if you wish, and then start assembly. Make up the end frames first. Measure diagonals to check symmetry. Join the frames with the lengthwise rails and check squareness of the parts by measuring diagonals while the legs are on a level surface.

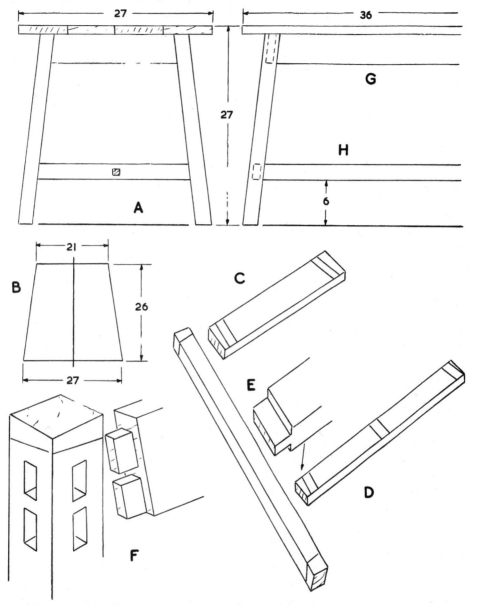

Fig. 6-4. The corners of the legs cover the same area as the top. End assemblies are tenoned first, and then the lengthwise rails added.

8. The boards for the top can be put on without joining their edges, but it would be better to make them up into a solid piece. That can be done by simple gluing, using dowels, or by secret slot screwing (see Chapter 2). Prepare the top as a unit, with rounded edges and corners, and then fit it to the framework by screwing downward or by one of the methods of attaching from below.

9. Finish the woodwork with paint, varnish, or preservative.

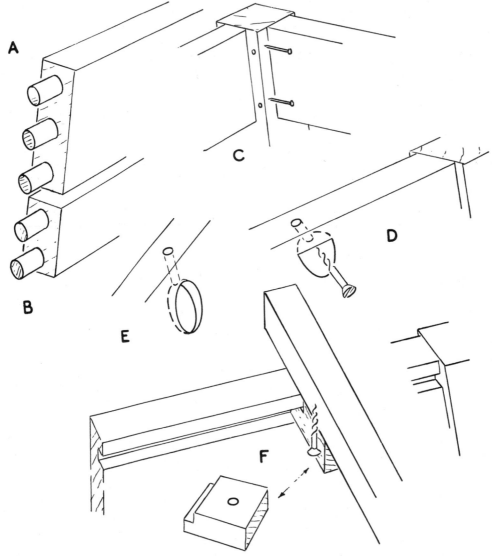

Fig. 6-5. Dowels could be used instead of tenons. The top can be held with slot screws or buttons.

OVAL-TOP TABLE

Curves soften appearance as well as remove sharp corners that might be dangerous or inconvenient. Any curve can be used and parts of circles are common, but ovals are considered more aesthetically pleasing. If you are making a tabletop that measures the same both ways, you can use a circle. If it is longer one way, the circle is stretched to an oval. This is more correctly called an *ellipse* because oval means egg-shaped (wider at one end).

A table with an oval top (Fig. 6-6) could be made any size and with various leg arrangements. Figure 6-6 shows splayed slab legs. A bottom rail is arranged

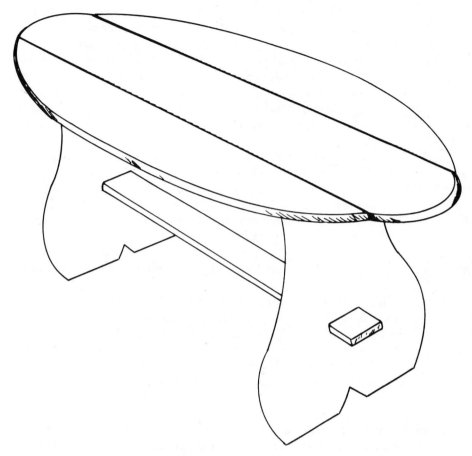

Fig. 6-6. An oval top gives an attractive shape to a table.

Materials List for Oval-top Table

2 legs	25	×	18	×	1½	
2 rails	40	×	4	×	1½	
1 top	40	×	20	×	1½	
2 wedges	8	×	1½	×	1¼	

flat so that it can be used as a shelf. The drawings show a similar table, but with the lower rail on edge. Using tusk tenons for that rail allows the assembly to be pulled tight even after swelling or shrinkage due to changes in the weather. The table is not meant to be dismantled.

The best wood is fairly thick hardwood and 1¼ inch or 1½ inch is suggested. Softwood could be used, but it would not have as long a life. The table shown in Fig. 6-6 has a top made up of three boards with battens across and gaps between. It would be better to join the board edges so that the top can be treated as a single piece when marking out the shape. With separate boards, expansion and contraction will show an unevenness in the outline at the joints.

The legs will also have to be made up of several boards joined together. Avoid having a joint line through the mortise and top notch. Whether the wood is planed or not depends on the situation. For a more rural part of the yard or garden, a sawn finish is appropriate. On a patio or deck, a smooth planed finish would be better. If the table is to make a set with tusk-tenoned chairs or benches, finish it in the same way.

1. Draw the main lines of the side view (Fig. 6-7A) to get the length and angles of the legs. The sizes given allow a slope of 15 degrees and bring the bottoms of the legs not quite to the length of the top, but wide enough for stability.

2. Mark out the legs (Figs. 6-7B and 8A). Get the actual length from your full-size drawing. Bevel the tops and bottoms and cut the curves, but leave cutting the joints until the other parts are ready.

3. Make the top rail (Figs. 6-7C and 8B). It has to be cut with halving joints into the legs (Fig. 6-8C). It is cut back shorter than the top will be and is beveled (Fig. 6-7D).

4. Get the length between shoulders of the bottom rail from your drawing. Allow some excess length on the tenons until after cutting the wedge slots. The shoulders of the tenons must match the slopes of the legs. Cut the tenons to width (Fig. 6-7E). Make mortises to match in the legs.

5. Mark out the wedge slots. The inner end of the slot should be at the same angle as the leg, but cut at least 1/8 of an inch inside its surface so that the wedge can pull in tight without binding on it. The outer end of the slot can be square. Make the wedges (Fig. 6-8D) too long at first and bevel their inner surfaces to match the leg. Cut through the outside of the slot to the same slope as the wedges.

6. Try each tenon in its leg. Trim the wedges so that they project about the same amount each side of their tenon, but it is wise to assume that they will drive further during later adjustments. Trim the ends of the tenons.

7. Assemble the parts. Because of the slope of the halving joints, you will have to progressively enter the tenons and the halving joints. Do not try to fix one rail before the other. Glue the top rail in, but allow for the wedges alone tightening and holding the bottom rail.

8. Join boards for the top, with battens below, that will have to be notched or glued into the top rail, preferably with dowels or secret-slot screwing (see Chapter 2).

9. The top can be made as a full oval or an ellipse. That takes away quite a lot of wood at the corners when compared with a plain rectangular top. That might not matter, but if you want to have a rather bigger top area, while still retaining curves, you could mark parts of circles across the ends (Fig. 6-8E). A full semicircle on the ends would leave short lengths straight at each side, but avoid sharp corners (Fig. 6-8F). For a larger area, round the corners of a rectangle. (Fig. 6-8G).

10. An ellipse of this size can be marked with pencil and string. Draw centerlines both ways on the top (Fig. 6-8H). Take half the length of the long

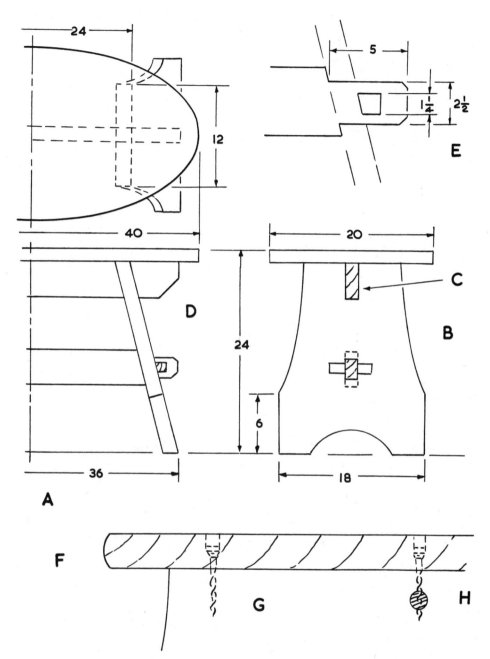

Fig. 6-7. *The framework of the oval table uses tusk tenons in the rails (A-E). The top can be screwed to the legs (F-H).*

centerline up to the top of the short line and measure this amount to a point on the long line (Fig. 6-8J). Measure the same the other way. Put nails or spikes at these points.

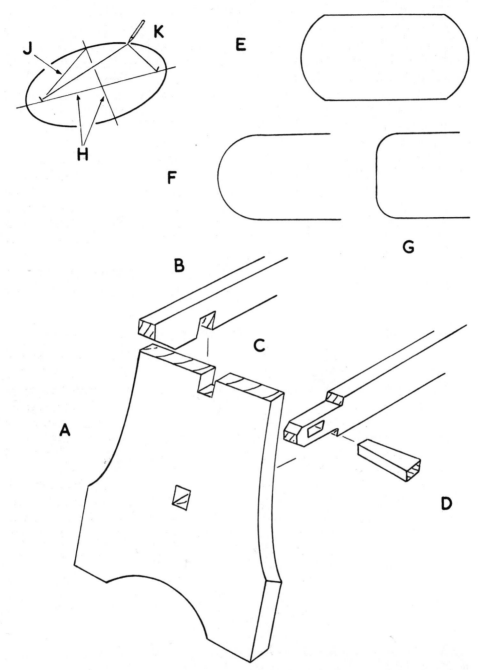

Fig. 6-8. Instead of an ellipse, there could be a parallel-sided top. Rails are notched and tenoned to the legs.

11. Make a loop by knotting a piece of nonstretch string, around the nails, long enough to reach the top mark on the short centerline. Put a pencil in the loop and take it round (Fig. 6-8K). Keep a tension on the string all the way and you will get a true ellipse. If you want to make the ellipse wider, bring the nails a little closer together. To make it longer move them further apart.

12. Cut the top to shape. It could be left with square edges, particularly if the surfaces are left sawn, but for a better finish it could have the edges semicircular. A flatter curve looks better (Fig. 6-7F). This could be done with a suitable router cutter or by careful planing and sanding.

13. It would be possible to attach the top with secret-slot screwing, as in the last project, but in the end grain of the legs this will not hold very well. It would probably be better to use secret-slot screwing along both sides of the top rail and counterbored and plugged screws into the legs (Fig. 6-7G), and with dowels across (Fig. 6-7H) if it is a type of wood that does not allow much grip for screws in end grain. Because the top and the legs both have grain the same way, any expansion and contraction should match easily.

14. Finish the table in a way to suit its situation. After it has been exposed to the weather for a few weeks, check the tightness of the wedges. Later checks will only be needed after prolonged changes in the weather.

SAWBUCK TABLE

A table with crossed legs would match the sawbuck chair described in the last chapter, but in itself it makes an attractive and interesting project (Fig. 6-9). The method of construction gives satisfactory bracing and a rigid table that might be considered more interesting visually than one with upright legs. There is slightly more wood in the legs, making the table heavier, but that could be an advantage where it is liable to be knocked and does not have to be moved often.

The wood used could be standard sections of softwood; hardwoods are also suitable. Whether the wood is left sawn or is planed depends on the situation. Sawn wood could have the main parts joined with bolts and screws used for joining the top and lengthwise rails. For a better table made of planed wood, the parts can be glued. They could also be screwed or bolted, but for an all-glued construction there might be dowels in nearly all joints. They could be taken right

---

Materials List for Sawbuck Table

4 legs	40	× 4	× 2
2 end rails	28	× 4	× 2
1 top rail	57	× 4	× 2
2 stretchers	53	× 4	× 2
2 top cleats	30	× 4	× 1
5 tops	60	× 5⅞	× 1

Fig. 6-9. A table with crossed sawbuck legs looks attractive in a yard.

through the leg-framing joints and would make an assembly of adequate strength for use on a patio or even indoors. The table would also have uses in a large greenhouse. The broad slatted top would make a good working bench or a stand for potted plants.

The sizes given are for a fairly large table of suitable size for meals. Use chairs of ordinary height. The same method of construction could be used for many other table sizes. This includes tiny tables for drinks and magazines alongside a chair. A small version would also be strong enough to use as a stool.

1. A full-size drawing of the main lines of an end is needed to obtain the sizes and shapes of the legs (Fig. 6-10A). They fit in a 27 inch square. At the ground the top edge meets the corner. At the other end it is 3 inches in from the corner. Draw the legs both ways and use this drawing to set them out and cut them.

2. It is inadvisable to make full-depth halving joints where the legs cross because that would weaken them too much. Nevertheless, some notching is advisable to keep them in correct relation under load. Mark where the legs cross and cut notches ¼ inch deep (Fig. 6-10B). During assembly, one ½-inch bolt through the center of the joint will pull the legs tight together and the notching will prevent movement.

3. The end rail, which goes across under the top (Fig. 6-10C and D), has to be brought square to the line of the table with a packing (which will be about

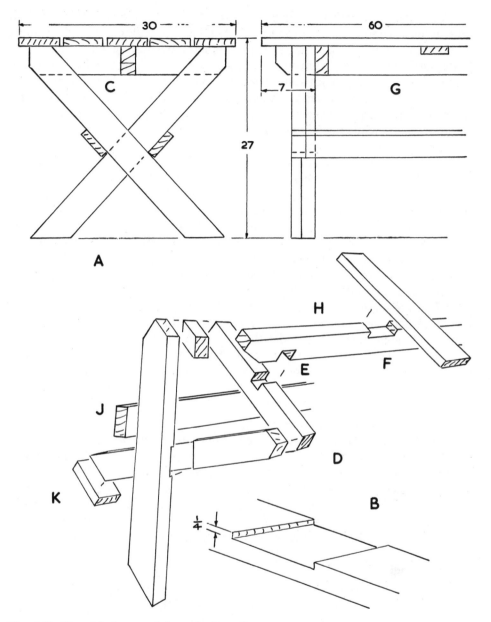

Fig. 6-10. The table framework is notched together.

1½ inch thick). Check what is needed by measuring the overlap on the actual legs. Mark a halving joint at the center of the rail for the lengthwise top rail (Fig. 6-10E). A ½-inch bolt through at each lap will join the legs to the end rail. Assemble these parts. If glued and doweled construction is being used, apply glue and clamp the joints while drilling for dowels. Four ½-inch dowels glued at each crossing should be sufficient.

4. Make the lengthwise top rail (Fig. 6-10F and G). Notch it to fit the end rails. If thick wood is used for the top, that will be still enough to hold its shape without further stiffening. Thinner boards should have bracing with cleats across underneath (Fig. 6-10H). Two evenly spaced cleats are suggested, but one at the center may be enough with some boards. Notch the top rail for the cleats.

5. The two stretchers are plain pieces screwed to the legs (Fig. 6-10J). Prepare them, and then complete assembly of the framework by fitting in the top rail and these stretchers while the legs are standing on a level surface and while you can see that the assembly is upright.

6. Any widths of boards can be used for the top, but there should be an odd number so that one covers the top rail. The suggested boards are a nominal 6 inches, which will probably be 5 ⅞ inches actual size (leaving gaps about ¼ inch wide). Take sharpness off the edges. Put the cleats in position. Screw the outside boards to the top end rails, and then space the others evenly between them and screw them in place. Either screw downward into the cleats or turn the table over and screw upward from the cleats into the boards. It will probably be sufficient to have the screw heads level on the top, but they can be counterbored and plugged for a better finish.

7. If the table is to stand on soft ground or you want to spread the load to reduce damage to a lawn surface, feet can be added. These could be offcuts from the stretchers screwed under the legs (Fig. 6-10K).

8. Round the corners and edges of the top, remove any roughness elsewhere and finish the wood to suit the situation for which it is to be used.

HEXAGONAL TABLE

Tables do not have to be rectangular. There is an attraction about sitting around a symmetrical table. If you want to use an umbrella shade on a central support, it is logical to shape the table around that central rod or tube. The table shown in Fig. 6-11 has a hexagonal top and three splayed legs, with a shelf underneath, so the top and the shelf provide bracing for the umbrella pole. With the three legs, there is the property of steadiness on an uneven surface. This will be an advantage if the umbrella is caught in a wind. Although the top is shown hexagonal, it could be made round with very little modification. The size and height should suit a meal or refreshments table with up to six people using chairs of normal height.

Materials List for Hexagonal Table				
3 legs	29	× 4	× 1	
3 top rails	12	× 4	× 1	
3 bottom rails	15	× 4	× 1	
2 center blocks	12	× 10	× 1	
6 top frames	22	× 2	× 1	
6 top borders	23	× 2	× 1	
1 top	40	× 35	× ½ plywood	
1 shelf	24	× 21	× ½ plywood	

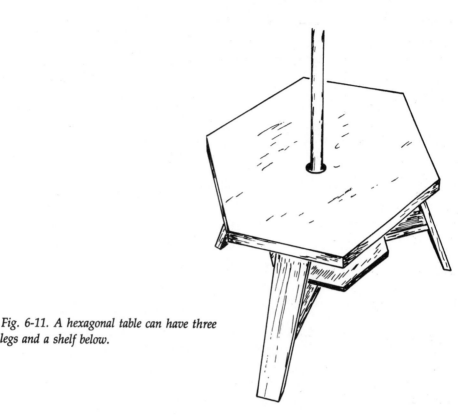

Fig. 6-11. A hexagonal table can have three legs and a shelf below.

The top and shelf are made of exterior-grade or marine-grade, ½ plywood. The other parts are all 1 inch thick. Construction should be easy with hand tools if power tools are unavailable. With a regular hexagonal shape, all the angles that have to be cut for the top framing are 60 degrees. Leg joint angles will be found on the drawing.

1. It will help in getting the sizes of many parts to have the top piece of plywood set out so that the underframing can be marked out on its underside. Its outline is obtained by drawing a circle, stepping off the radius around the circumference, and then joining these points. The plywood is bordered with wood 1 inch thick (Fig. 6-13A). A suitable circumference for the circle is about 38 inches.

2. On the underside of the top, mark another hexagon on a 12-inch circle (Fig. 6-12A). From this draw the outlines of the top rails to the centers of three sides (Fig. 6-12B).

3. Make a center block to this hexagonal shape. It is 1 inch thick, but you can use pieces to make up its size if you do not have a single piece of wood large enough. It will be glued and screwed to the top so that will reinforce any joints needed to make up width.

4. Fit the block to the top plywood and drill through for the umbrella pole. Make it an easy fit; 1½ inch will probably suit most poles (Fig. 6-13B).

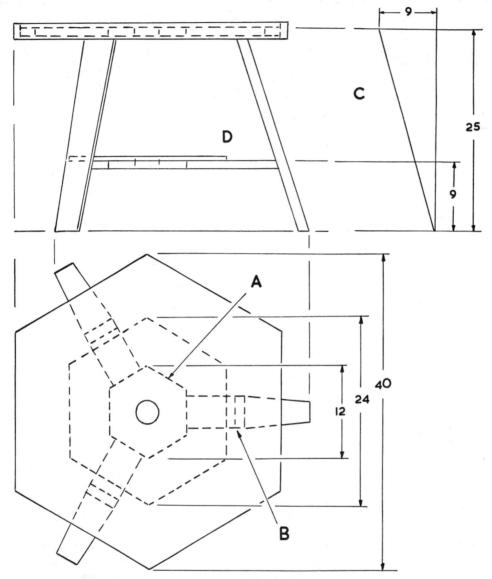

Fig. 6-12. The table shape is set from a pattern of regular hexagons.

5. Frame around the plywood top with strips underneath (Fig. 6-13C). Miter their corners. If you do not get a perfect fit, it does not matter. Aim to get the outer corners tight.

6. Cut the top rails (Fig. 6-13D) to fit in place, but do not fix them yet.

7. To obtain the shape and slope of the legs, set one out (Fig. 6-12C). From this cut the wood for the legs. Allow a little extra at the top for tenons. Taper the legs from just below the tenon shoulders to 3 inches wide at the bottom. Mark the mortise positions at what will be 6 inches in from the outside of the top (Fig.

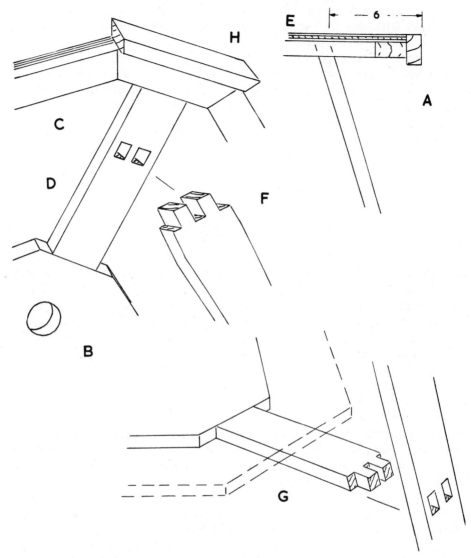

Fig. 6-13. Constructional details of the top and shelf of the hexagonal table.

6-13E). Mark and cut the mortise and tenon joints. A pair of tenons is advised (Fig. 6-13F). Do not assemble these parts yet.

8. At the shelf level, mark out in a very similar way to the top. Make the shelf (Fig. 6-12D). It can be left unframed unless you want to add a lip to prevent things from falling off.

9. On the underside of the shelf, fit a center block the same as that under the top, and drill through with the same size hole.

10. From the leg setting out get the length of the bottom rails. Each bottom rail has to fit against the center block and be tenoned to the leg in a similar way to the top joints (Fig. 6-13G).

11. Frame around the outside of the top with mitered strips (Fig. 6-13H). Attach them with glue and screws. Make sure the edges of the plywood are thoroughly glued so water is unlikely to enter the end grain of the veneers. Round the outer edges of the top when the glue has set.

12. With all the joints prepared, assemble the legs and rails. It is advisable to first join the legs to the top rails. Wedge the tenons from above and plane level before fitting the rails to the top. The bottom rail tenons can also be wedged, but you can do that during assembly.

13. Check that all legs splay the same amount by comparing the angles they make with the top or shelf. Before the glue has set, view the table from above to see that all legs project the same amount. Stand back and look at the table from several directions to check its symmetrical appearance.

14. A painted finish is most appropriate.

PICNIC TABLE

Picnic tables are found everywhere from wayside rest areas to campgrounds, parks, and anywhere that people want to eat outdoors—including yards and gardens. The ubiquitous picnic table tends to follow a standard pattern. If you look at the details of the better ones, construction is basically the same. Sizes differ, but the way they are made does not vary much. The usual picnic table with built-in side benches has splayed legs at the ends, crosspieces to support the bench tops, and there should be some lengthwise bracing.

This picnic table is of moderate size, intended to be fairly heavy (and therefore stable), and it follows the common pattern (Fig. 6-14). Its sizes could be varied. As shown it provides roomy seating for at least six adults at a comfortable height. The end view (Fig. 6-15A) would be the same for any length, unless the wood sizes are altered considerably. If the table is made much longer, there should be one or more cleats across under the top boards and possibly under the seats. If longer seats become too flexible, they will need similar diagonal bracing to the tabletop.

All of the parts in this project are 2-inch-by-4-inch section. They might be left as sawn, but will be better planed when the sections will be about $\frac{1}{8}$ inch undersize. The seven pieces making up the tabletop should have narrow gaps between them for drainage. Try the wood you have for total width and vary the size a little if necessary.

The main parts could be bolted together. One $\frac{5}{8}$-inch bolt through the center of each joint should be enough. Alternatively, use two thinner ones, such as $\frac{3}{8}$-

Materials List for Picnic Table						
4 legs	38	×	4	×	2
2 seat rails	52	×	4	×	2
2 top rails	27	×	4	×	2
4 seats	54	×	4	×	2
7 tops	48	×	4	×	2
2 struts	33	×	4	×	2

Fig. 6-14. A picnic table with built-in benches fits into any yard.

arranged diagonally across a joint so that the holes do not come in the same grain lines and possibly cause splits. The top and seat boards can be nailed on or screwed. If nailed, the heads should be punched below the surface and covered with stopping. Screws are best counterbored and plugged.

1. The only setting out needed is to obtain and measure the splay of the legs. The exact slopes are not crucial, but obviously they should be the same both ways. The measurements on the end view (Fig. 6-15A) will allow you to set out the main lines of the legs. At their tops they are 2 inches apart (Fig. 6-15B) and at the bottom they spread to 48 inches (Fig. 6-15C). Although shown taken to a fine edge at the bottom, the outer corner should be cut and rounded to minimize the risk of the wood splintering. Make the legs (Fig. 6-16A) from your drawing. Mark on them where the seat rail will cross.

2. Make the top rails (Figs. 6-15D) and 6-16B) a little shorter than the overall width of the top will be and bevel the undersides of their ends.

3. Make the seat rails (Figs.6-15E and 6-16C). If there are any variations in quality, choose your straightest wood for these parts.

4. With your full-size setting out as a guide, put the parts of an end together and drill through for bolts. There could be waterproof glue in each joint, but the bolts alone should be secure enough. Without glue, it is advisable with most woods to coat the meeting surfaces with preservative. Use the first assembled end as a guide when assembling the other end as a pair to it.

5. Prepare the boards for the top and seats. Take sharpness off the edges and round the ends (either now or after assembly). Outer corners of the seats and top should be well rounded.

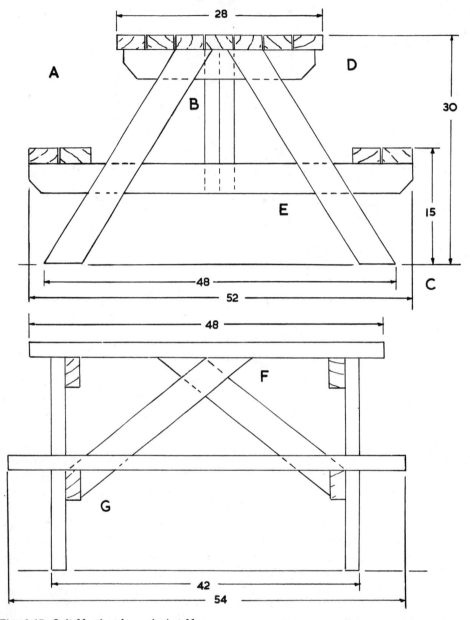

Fig. 6-15. Suitable sizes for a picnic table.

6. Mark on the undersides of these boards where the end frames will come and drill for screws or nails.

7. Make a first assembly with the ends standing on a level surface for getting the shapes of the diagonal struts. Fit the center top board and one seat board at each side. Check that the ends are standing upright and squarely in relation to the boards you have fitted.

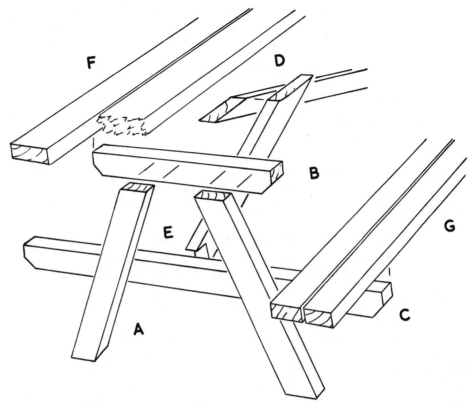

Fig. 6-16. The relative positions of parts in a picnic table.

8. The two struts have their top edges meeting at the center of the top board. They overlap and will be bolted through (Figs. 6-15F and 6-16D). At their lower ends, the top surfaces should extend to the outsides of the seat rails, and then have notches to fit over (Figs. 6-15G and 6-16E).

9. Make the two struts. It is possible to make small adjustments by sliding the overlapping tops over each other until they fit closely at both ends while the framework is standing true. When you are satisfied, bolt the struts to each other and screw down into their tops through the top board. At their bottoms screw or nail in place.

10. Fit the other top and seat boards (Fig. 6-16F and G). A short piece of thin wood is a good guide to make gaps all the same width. Make sure all screws and bolts are as tight as possible. Washers under the bolt heads and nuts will prevent them from pulling in.

11. The finished picnic table could be painted, but for leaving outside indefinitely it is best treated with preservative—which is renewed occasionally.

7
CHAPTER

Fences
and Gates

A wide-open vista at the limit of your property can be attractive, both for you looking out and for possible admirers looking in, but in many cases it is necessary to mark the limit of your land and to keep out trespassers and animals. In particular, straying animals, whether domestic or wild, can wreck your carefully nurtured flower beds or kill off your growing vegetables. This means that for at least part of your garden you need fences. If you have a fence, you must have some means of getting through or over it that is equally animal-proof. Usually there is a door or gate, but perhaps a stile will be appropriate in some situations.

Medieval owners of stately homes used one alternative to a fence and that was a ditch. They could sit and look over their garden into the farmland beyond, but cattle from the farm could not cross the ditch into the garden. Obviously this ditch, which was picturesquely called a *ha-ha*, had to be fairly wide and deep if the cows were to be discouraged. You might not have the space or energy to make such a ditch, but a smaller ditch might be worth considering to impede smaller animals. If you need to drain water away, the ditch could serve that purpose as well.

Fences can be made in many ways and to different sizes. A few strands of wire stretched between posts would keep out larger animals and show people where the boundary is without having much effect on the view. A solid fence would also protect against animals and would be a windbreak. If you want privacy as well, the solid fence should be at least 6 feet high. If you want to keep geese or smaller animals from a vegetable garden, you need a fairly close mesh wire netting if you are not to build a solid fence.

The fences most of us build will be wood because we have the facilities for working it and are familiar with the techniques. For many purposes a wood fence is perfectly satisfactory. The vulnerable part is where wood posts go into the

136

ground. There they can become loose and will be subject to rot. A better arrangement uses concrete posts for the full height or far enough above the ground for the wood posts to be bolted to them.

Some fences are wholly or partially made of metal. Corrugated metal sheeting can be mounted on wood or metal framing. Corrugated or flat plastic sheeting could be used. Some of it will let sunlight through while providing a wind screen and some privacy.

The most solid fence is a wall built of stone. If stone is plentiful it makes a very attractive fence that usually fits in better with its surroundings than any of the other types. If sufficient stone has to be brought from a distance, cost would probably rule it out. Brick can be used in a very similar way, but it has a regular pattern of courses that will suit some situations; hence, it tends to be too prominent in others. Concrete can be used alone or with prepared blocks. Finishing it with a stonelike surface disguises its often stark appearance.

Another type of fence is a grown hedge. It takes time to grow, but it can be decorative as a natural-looking boundary marker. The best type of plants or shrubs for the soil and locality will have to be chosen. It is possible to grow a high windbreak, a low arrangement of widely spaced plants or trees, or an almost impenetrable mass of intertwined branches and twigs. You will probably have to start with an arrangement of stakes, possibly with a few horizontal rails or wires, to serve as a foundation for the hedge as it grows. That arrangement will disappear inside the mass of foliage as it develops.

A stile can be made with any type of fence by providing steps on each side with built-up wood, projecting stones, or cast concrete. Gates are mostly wood. Metal gates are possible if you have facilities for welding, but a gate can put a considerable load on its hinges and there is an advantage in the comparative lightness of wood. Wood will also usually look better and can provide a decorative feature in an otherwise rather plain fence. An exception is a wrought-iron gate with its many curls and scrolls, but not many of us are smiths capable of making one of these.

For the entrance to your property, it is possible to fashion very elaborate gates. A pair of attractive gates will make a good impression on visitors as they turn into your drive (even if the gates are open most of the time).

POST TOOLS

If you want to build a fence with stone or brick, you have to dig a trench for foundations. This is straightforward hard work with pick and spade or, more likely today, a quick job with a hired excavator.

There are just a few wood fence methods that do not involve posts entering the ground some way, but for most fences you have to erect posts. So that they will stay upright indefinitely and not succumb to wind or other pressure on the fence, they should go into the soil quite deeply. How deep depends on the soil, but you should regard 18 inches as the minimum for a fence standing waist high, and go deeper for a high fence or softer soil.

It is very unlikely that a pointed post could be driven in by hand methods without a hole being made first. There are post drivers mounted on tractors for farm work that will push a post into the most stubborn ground. If you can get the use of one of these and the tractor will not damage your garden, it could be the answer to your post-driving problem.

Dig the hole with an ordinary spade. The hole would be much bigger than the post. The post is then placed in position and the soil is put back and tamped down tightly around it. There are narrow, long-bladed spades made for this purpose so that you do not have to cut away quite such a large area. There could be a combination of digging and driving, with the spade used to make a hole and loosen the soil left in, and then the post driven and tamped firmly. If you only have a few posts to erect and no special tools, this is a satisfactory method.

There are posthole borers of several types that are intended to remove soil from a hole not much further across than the size of the post. They can be successful if you have only soil to remove. If there are stones where the post is to come, you will still have to dig to remove them.

One type of borer is like a large auger. Blades cut their way into the soil and lift it (Fig. 7-1A). As the tool is withdrawn, it lifts the loose soil from the hole. A hand auger will have a cross handle to give plenty of leverage. A similar cutter can be power driven, and either self-contained or mounted on a tractor. Another type has a pair of scooped blades operated with handles something like scissors (Fig. 7-1B). The tool is thrust into the ground. Handles are moved to pinch the soil between the blades so it can be lifted out, ready for another thrust to deepen the hole.

Ideally both tools should make a hole slightly smaller than the post—which is usually square—so it forces its way in and becomes tight without further attention. If the hole is larger, as it often is, you have to do some further tamping or you can pack around the post with strips of wood to make up size. If you do that, the packing should be as durable as the post, treated with preservative, and not just oddments you pick up. The wood could rot and give you trouble later on.

Fence posts should normally be pointed, but if you are digging a hole as deep as the pole is to go, a full size square end has the advantage of being less likely to sink deeper after the fence has been assembled. Sinkage of a post in soft ground could spoil the appearance of the finished fence. In most ground a point is an advantage. Do not cut to a fine point; it could crumble. An end about ¾ of an inch across would be better. The angle of the end is not crucial and a length of 6 inches on a 4-inch post is reasonable for most soils (Fig. 7-1C). Usually the taper is square whether the post is round or square. It could be sawn or chopped with an ax.

Drive a post with the heaviest hammer you can handle. An outsize mallet, called a maul (made by putting a piece of tree trunk on a handle), is also effective and less likely to split the post. In any case, the post should be too long and a piece of scrap wood is held over its end to take hammer blows.

Hammering involves someone holding the post. Apart from any risk of damage to them, it is difficult to keep the post upright. A one- or two-man tool, less hazardous and easier to keep on course, is made from a piece of heavy steel tubing that will slip over the post and an end welded in. Two handles are welded on

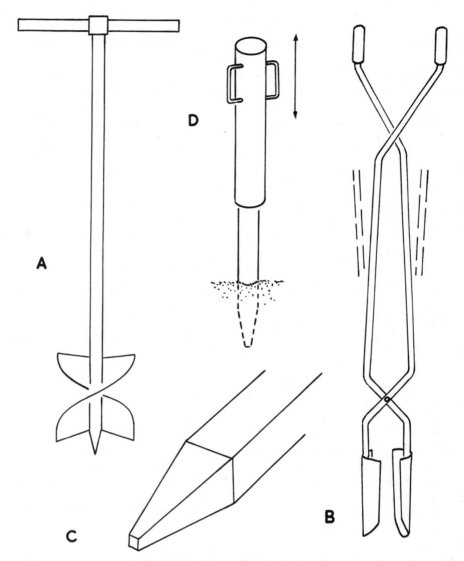

Fig. 7-1. Posthole borers (A,B) make holes with less disturbance than digging with a spade. A point makes driving easier (C). A tube for pounding is better than a hammer (D).

and the tube is pounded up and down by a pair of workers (Fig. 7-1D). Its weight and fit are more effective than hammering.

A large pointed round steel rod, about 36 inches long and 1 inch in diameter, is useful for starting holes, levering out stones, and penetrating the ground. A flat steel rod about the same length and maybe 2-inch-by-½-inch section, with its end thinned, can be used like a chisel to square holes or use as a lever. For tamping down soil around a post, a tool consisting of a block of iron on the end of a handle could be used. A piece of fence post with its end cut square across is almost as good.

WIRE TOOLS

If a fence is made in any of the ways that use wood rails and other wood parts, the tools needed are only those used for other types of carpentry. Many fences are made with wires between posts supporting netting or other meshes to stop animals or birds. The horizontal wires have to be pulled fairly tight, and various tools and techniques have been devised for this purpose. It is unlikely that barbed wire will be used unless your garden adjoins farm land. The tools and techniques devised by farmers for dealing with barbed wire, as well as those used by telegraph workers for attaching wires to posts, can be of use in the more modest attaching of plain wire to posts around a yard or garden.

Wire can be attached to posts with staples. Special manufactured tensioning devices mostly provide a lever action for the second end post. If the wire is brought through a hole, it could be given a turn around a strip of wood and pulled to tighten it (Fig. 7-2A). You have to be ready to secure the wire with staples, but a small vise can be put on the wire to prevent it pulling back through the hole (Fig. 7-2B) while you do this. Putting a turn of stiff wire round the lever can be difficult. An alternative is an acutely notched steel plate on the lever (Fig. 7-2C). If the wire is held down in the notch, the steel will grip the wire well enough while levering.

If the wire comes on the face of the end post, it can be strained over the edge and staples can be driven there before releasing the lever to allow more staples to be driven further round (Fig. 7-2D).

Another way of tensioning uses a grip on the wire further from the post. Manufactured devices for this purpose use one of many types of grip, including a vise action. Any small hand or metalworking vise could be used. A wire grip could be used, possibly with a short length of spare wire included to make up the thickness (Fig. 7-2E), and then a tackle made up of two blocks and strong rope is attached and used to pull the wire toward the post (Fig. 7-2F). With the tension on, you can deal with stapling with more space to move around the post than with the other methods.

Stapling can be done with your normal hammer, pliers and a screwdriver, to lever out staples that go wrong.

PRIMITIVE FENCES

Where the early settlers had an abundance of wood left from clearing land, they devised fences that used poles laid in a zigzag form, without any posts or stakes into the ground in the simplest versions. Where the felled logs were too thick to use as they were, they were split into two or four. The method certainly uses a considerable amount of wood. One early authority said that a fence of this type 10 rails high, using poles about 11 feet long, needed 8000 rails to the mile. Even for the more modest confines of a home garden, there would have to be a great many poles. If you want to provide a fence that reflects traditional form and have enough poles available, this is an interesting project even if you only build a token fence for a short distance (Fig. 7-3A).

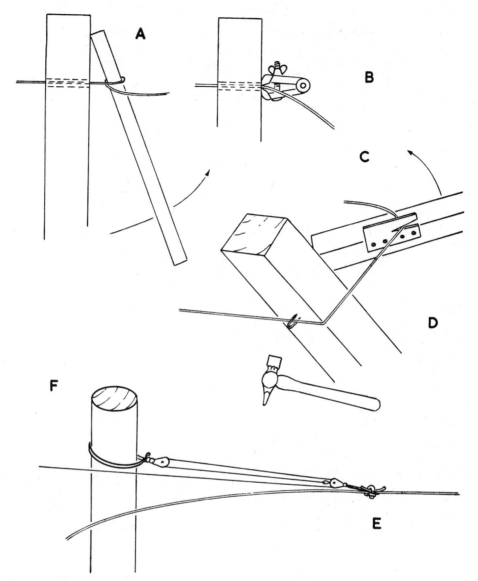

Fig. 7-2. Fence wires can be strained in several ways.

If you want to mark the limits of your property or a particular part of it, without the need to restrict animals, this type of fence could be made only three or four poles high and the poles need not be as long as they would be for farm fencing. The result would be visually attractive.

To lay out such a fence, get together a stock of poles, either fully round, from about 3 inch diameter upward, or large ones split to about that size. The fence looks best if all poles are about the same size, but you can graduate sizes from the bottom upward. Decide on the length of poles and cut them all to size. You

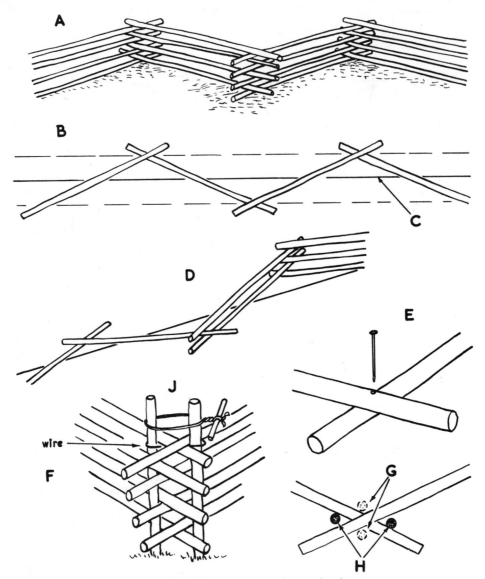

Fig. 7-3. Primitive fences are made with poles supported on each other.

vary panels to suit poles, but if the fence is to extend very far it will look best with panels of even size. You have to allow for overlaps. Suppose your poles are 10 feet long. They will overlap about 18 inches; the actual length covered by each panel is about 7 feet. If you have definite space to fill, work out panel lengths to suit.

You can lay out the fence with the bottom poles overlapped until you are satisfied with the experiment. For farm fences, the width of the zigzag arrangement was about half the length of a panel (Fig. 7-3B). If the fence is to be straight, it is a help to put down a central string (Fig. 7-3C) and arrange the crossings fairly regularly each side of it.

You can build up a little at a time all the way along, but if there is much length it is less laborious to work progressively from one end (Fig. 7-3D). Traditionally, the poles were just laid there. If you want to be more certain of the poles staying in place, you can drive a long nail down through the crossings as they are made (Fig. 7-3E).

If your fence is only the 12 inches or so high of a four-rail assembly, that will probably be all you want to do. The next step used by the settlers to make the fence stronger, without nails, was to drive in stakes where the poles cross. Stakes should be taller than the fence is to go, and they are driven in after two or three poles crossing have shown their positions. When the fence has reached the height you want, the poles are pulled together with wire below the top pair (Fig. 7-3F). The stakes could come in either of the opposite angles (Fig. 7-3G and H). The best way to get the grip tight is to pull the tops of the poles together with a clamp or a Spanish windlass, made by putting a loop of rope around the poles and twisting with a stick (Fig. 7-3J). While the pressure is on, tie the wire tightly and inconspicuously in the gap below. Remove the Spanish windlass. Nail in the two top poles, if you prefer, and cut off the tops of the stakes level.

Several other methods of strengthening farm fences of this type were used, but they involved supports set sawbuck fashion so they project each side. This could be an obstruction and nuisance in a garden.

RAIL AND POST FENCE

Rails nailed to posts have developed from the widely spaced rails of a farm fence (Fig. 7-4A) to the neater and more closely spaced fence of planed boards used around home property (Fig. 7-4B). For a board or rail fence, posts should not not be more than 8 feet apart and could be down to no more than 5 feet. A closer arrangement of posts makes for stability and rigidity of the boards. This might warp and spoil appearance if used over a longer span.

If the fence is to be straight, set out the positions of postholes with a cord line (Fig. 7-5A) and use the line frequently as you progress to erecting the posts. It helps to sight along as well. If you look along a row of posts from one end, you can easily see any post that is out of line or not plumb. The further you can stand back to sight, the easier it is to see errors.

Make the postholes by any method described earlier. If the posts are to go directly into the soil, very thoroughly soak their lower ends in preservative. Creosote is often used, but there are many suitable prepared preservatives. Tamp the soil tightly around each post. Stones rammed in will help tighten the post.

If the post is to be set in concrete, treat its bottom with preservative as if for driving into soil. Have the hole reasonably parallel and about three times the size of the post (Fig. 7-5B). Set the post on stones for drainage and pour and ram concrete tightly into place. Trowel the top so any water is shed away from the wood (Fig. 7-5C). Check for plumb as you work. Correcting after the concrete has set is almost impossible.

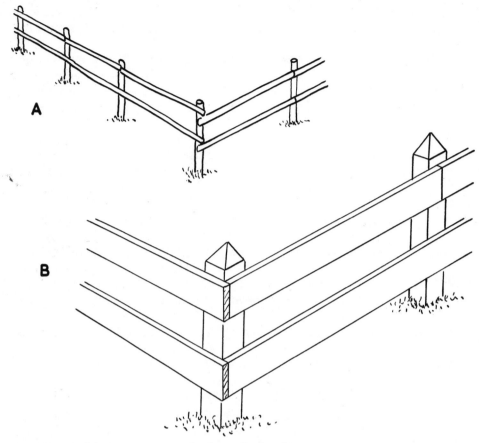

Fig. 7-4. A rail fence can use natural poles or flat boards.

If the wood post is to be attached to a concrete post set in the ground, you may cast your own post or suitable ones can be bought. Although the concrete post could go directly into soil, it is better to set it into concrete. Then the wood post is bolted on with its foot above ground level (Fig. 7-5D).

For a yard fence, the posts could be 3 inches or more square with planed surfaces if the wood is to be painted. For a farm fence or more primitive fence, the wood need not be planed and it could be round or square. If a fence is liable to get thrusts square to it (from cattle or even a car backing into it), the posts could be thicker. You could have a 3-inch face against the boards and 6 inches or more the other way.

The boards could be any convenient width, but narrow widths will be too flexible for strength between supports. They need not all be the same width. For a three-rail fence, you could have 6 inches at the top and the others 5 inches and 4 inches (Fig. 7-5E). Thickness should usually be at least 1 inch. Obviously, you must avoid boards with large knots that would weaken them. If possible, have the boards long enough to continue to a second post. Joints can be staggered

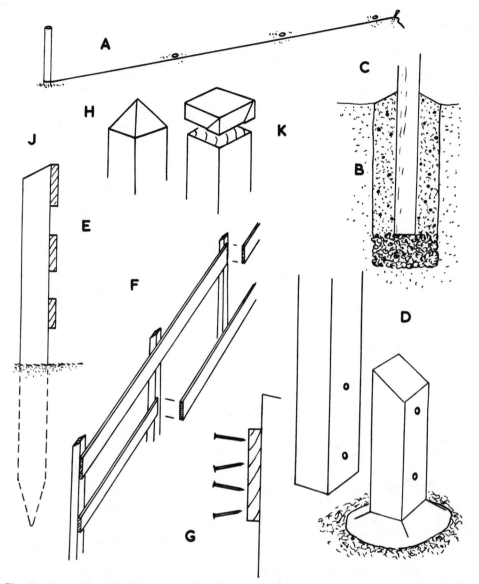

Fig. 7-5. Fence holes should be marked straight (A) and posts can be set in or attached to concrete (B-D). Nail boards to posts (E-G). Shape or cover post tops (H-K).

(Fig. 7-5F). Let board ends meet closely and use sufficient nails; four in a 6 inch width should be satisfactory (Fig. 7-5G).

To get the boards level, use a stretched string. Preferably, it should be from one extreme of the fence to the other. If it is very long, you might have to level in stages. Check the top board level first. Waviness in the top edge of a fence becomes very obvious to a viewer. From the string, mark on each post where the board should come. Even then it is advisable to first fit each board with one nail only at each crossing, then stand back and see that the top edge makes a continuous level line.

With the top boards level, the others can be measured down from them. The post tops can be cut level with the boards or they can be allowed to project. Unless they are to be covered in some way, they should slope so water drains off instead of soaking into grain. Projecting posts can be taken to a point (Fig. 7-5H). Cut to a single slope whether they finish level with the boards or project (Fig. 7-5J). To completely prevent water from entering the end grain, thin sheet metal can be folded over and tacked on (Fig. 7-5K).

A board attached flat above the top vertical board can also cover the tops of the posts, making an attractive capping that gives a more solid appearance to

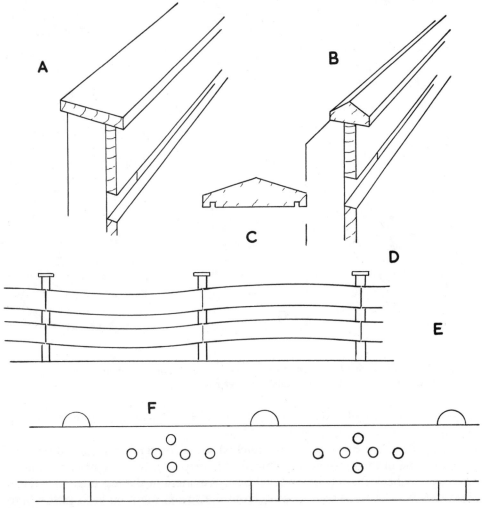

Fig. 7-6. Clapping and decoration are possible on rail fences.

the fence (Fig. 7-6A). Just a square over a post would have similar effect (Fig. 7-6D). If you do not want such a wide top, there could be a narrower shaped piece (Fig. 7-6B), taken partly over each post top, which is sloped outside it. Water has a tendency to run back underneath an overhang. It will not matter on a fence, but is can be prevented by plowing a groove a short distance from the edge (Fig. 7-6C).

Boards in this type of fence do not have to be left plain. They could be cut with curved outlines (Fig. 7-6E). They could be drilled or pierced (Fig. 7-6F). Painting rails in different colors can be distinctive.

If the fence is to have a painted finish, any wood that is not inherently durable should be treated with a preservative that can be covered with paint.

MORTISED FENCE

Instead of nailing rails to the surface of posts, they can be let into mortises. It is not easy cutting mortises in posts that have been erected. The method is better suited to positions where the posts can be prepared in advance and erected to the correct height in holes that allow them to be adjusted with packing stones or other means before tamping tight. The method can be used with natural wood or sawn boards. Cleft poles make good rails for this type of fence (Fig. 7-7).

Round rails, probably no more than 3 inches in diameter, could be used with posts 5 inches in diameter or square. Poles could be cleft along their centers and the fence built with all the flat surfaces to one side. If the fence is to withstand cows or horses pushing against it, the cleft poles could be up to 6 inches in diameter (particularly for the top rails). If you want a natural, rural look to the garden fence, you can use rather lighter posts and rails to get the same effect. The poles do not have to be straight, and a fence of this sort with rails giving a slightly uneven appearance will look right if it separates the cultivated garden from a background of trees and bushes that have been left to nature.

If flat boards are used, they can be planed and painted in the same way as a nailed fence or they can be left as sawn and treated with preservative for a more natural appearance. Strength in the joints comes from having the posts fairly thick in relation to the rails, this is particularly important if you are using flat boards. This is less important, although still valuable, with round or cleft rails in a fence where the haphazard appearance of extending rail ends does not matter and may even be considered a feature.

1. For a fence with round or split rails, assemble the materials for the rails. These will determine the spacing of posts. Allow for overlaps at the joints. Short rails and more frequent posts will have the best resistance to sideways pressures. If it is only a garden fence where the loads will not be much, you can have the poles any reasonable length. Depending on the type of wood, bark can be removed or left on; it will not affect construction.

2. The posts are best left longer than you need them eventually, and with sufficient length to go into the ground. Point them if they are to be driven, or leave them square if they will be set in dug holes. If the ground where the fence will be is uneven and you want the rails to be horizontal, work to the highest level and make the posts longer for the lower parts.

Fig. 7-7. With a mortised fence, the rails can fit against each other.

3. The ends of split rails have to be reduced to a rectangular section (Fig. 7-8A). What this size will be depends on the wood, but you have to compromise between width and depth. A thickness about 1½ inches and depth of 2½ inches might be possible and is the proportion at which to aim. Do not reduce the ends too much, but the reduced size should extend for about the thickness of a post. Experiment with your poles or with offcuts to get a size that will suit your stock of rails. Precision is not important, but try to keep close to the size on which you settle. Reduce round rails from both sides (Fig. 7-8B). Tapering can be done with a saw, ax, or drawknife.

4. In the posts, the mortises should suit the thickness you are making the rails and be rather deeper than them. If the rails are 2½ inches deep, the mortises

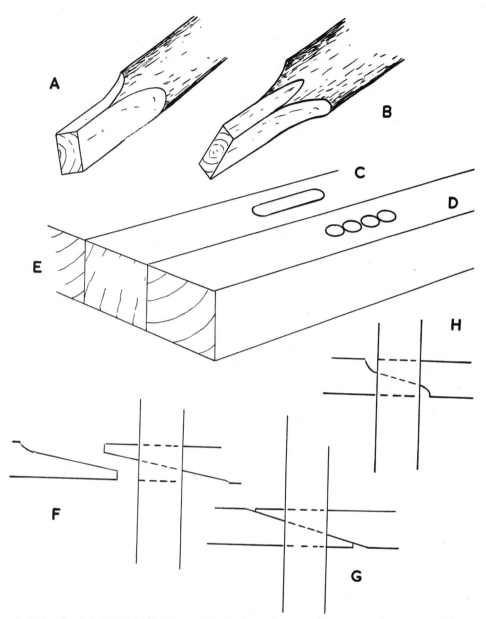

Fig. 7-8. Shape rail ends to fit the mortises in the posts.

could be 3½ inches (Fig. 7-8C). They need not be chopped square and are best made by drilling several holes and removing the waste (Fig. 7-8D) with a chisel. Roughness and unevenness inside a mortise will not matter. Prepare posts in groups so mortise spacings match (Fig. 7-8E).

5. When you erect the fence, work along it by positioning posts loosely in their holes so you can move them a little. Add rails from one end and tighten

the posts in the ground after their rails are fixed. At each post, the rails should be tapered to fit each other (Fig. 7-8F) so when they are forced tight they press against the top and bottom of the mortise. It is advisable to make the edge tapers as you go so that each one can allow for slight variations of the previous one and you may have to make some length adjustments. The ends that extend through could be left (Fig. 7-8G) or cut off at the post (Fig. 7-8H). If the ends are to be left, try to avoid tapering to a feather edge. It is better to leave ½ inch or so.

6. In a natural fence, there should be no need to do any more, but if joints shrink and loosen you can nail through the mortise.

7. If flat boards are to be used for rails, the method of assembly is very similar. Their thickness will settle the width of the mortises. If the depth of a rail is no more than the thickness of the post, there is no need to reduce it (Fig. 7-9A). If it is deeper, there will have to be a shoulder at one or both edges (Fig. 7-9B).

8. The mortises can still be made by drilling (and left with rounded ends and the rails eased a little with a chisel), or you can chop the ends square (Fig. 7-9C).

9. The rails can have their ends cut to go through in a very similar way to the natural poles (Fig. 7-9D) or they can be angled to fit each other within the thickness (Fig. 7-9E). The second method is neater, but the joints will have to be secured with dowels (Fig. 7-9F).

10. It is unlikely that posts will be erected with the precision of spacing that you would expect in cabinetry. Differences of an inch or so do not matter, but this means that rails should be cut after the posts are loosely positioned, particularly if you will be making shoulders on them. Measure the distances between posts at ground level and use this as the distance between them where the rails will be.

11. In both methods of construction, get the fence erected with all posts still too long. When you are satisfied that it is as you want it, cut the tops off the posts—either at an angle or to a point.

PICKET FENCE

Probably the most common traditional garden fence has posts and rails, but between the posts are upright pieces attached to the rails. The whole fence can be quite low; it is commonly about waist-high, or it could be high enough to provide some privacy or act as a windbreak.

The variations are almost limitless. The upright pickets can be narrow or wide; they can almost touch or be wide apart; they could be on two, three or more rails. Instead of flat pieces, they could be round or square; the tops could be cut square or decorated, or they may be sloping instead of upright. In building a picket fence, there is scope for you to express your individuality. The instructions here are for straightforward picket fences of conventional design (Fig. 7-10) that can be adapted to suit your needs and ideas.

1. Measure the place the fence is to be and decide on a suitable post spacing. If the fence is not expected to have to withstand much load, the posts can be

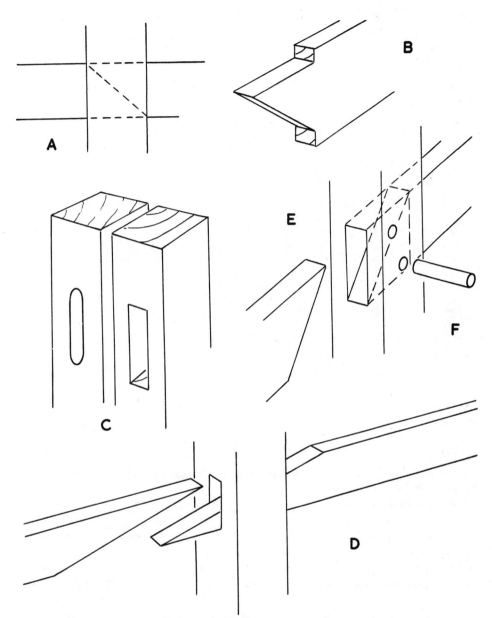

Fig. 7-9. Flat rails should fit together in the mortises.

wider apart than if you expect there to be occasional bumps. If the fence is to be at the boundary of your property and a public path or road, it is advisable to assume there could be unexpected occasional heavy loads.

2. If the fence is to keep in children, do not have spaces greater than 3 inches wide. This will also do for the majority of animals.

3. The number of rails depends on the height of the fence. Two rails should suit pickets standing 36 inches high or anything below that. If you are using light

Fig. 7-10. A picket fence suits most gardens.

rods or other special pieces for pickets, there will have to be a third rail—even at this height.

4. The simplest way to make the fence is to nail the rails to the posts and the pickets to the rails, but this brings the pickets forward (Fig. 7-11A). To keep the appearance even along the fence, you must keep the posts inconspicuous and continue pickets over them (Fig. 7-11B).

5. Another way is to mortise the rails into the posts so the outside surfaces of the pickets will be level with the surfaces of the posts (Fig. 7-11C). The posts then form part of a line with the pickets and their tops can be decorated, in the same way, whether they stand up or are level with them (Fig. 7-11D).

6. For a waist-high garden fence, the posts might be about 4 inches square and the rails 2 inches square. It helps to slope the top of each rail (Fig. 7-11E) so that rainwater runs off instead of becoming trapped between the rail and the pickets (where rot could start). Even better is to use rails made by cutting diagonally across a square piece (Fig. 7-11F). To be as strong as 2 inches square, the wood cut should be 3 inches or more square. Rain is unlikely to be trapped behind such an *arris rail*.

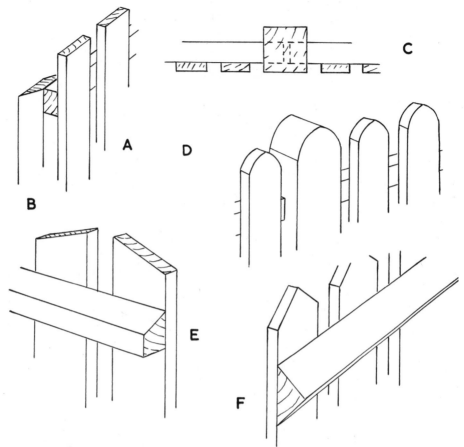

Fig. 7-11. Picket fence details can be varied to suit requirements.

7. Arrange the rail heights to suit your proposed design (Fig. 7-12A). The bottoms of the pickets should be clear of the ground. If you need to retain soil, a horizontal board could be used below the pickets (Fig. 7-12B). That might be regarded as expendable because it will probably rot. It could be nailed to the posts so that it is easily removed and replaced.

8. The widths of pickets can be anything from 2 inches up to 6 inches and will depend on what is available. Widths can vary. One wide picket between a regular series of narrower ones will be distinctive. You have to scheme out the spacing along the rails. Distances between posts should be kept the same or you will get different spacings. This will show when the fence is viewed from a distance. If there have to be different post spacings, work them out so that they are proportional and pickets will still have the same gaps. Pickets can be from ½ inch thick upward, but ¾ inch to 1 inch is usual.

9. Use two nails at each crossing and arrange them diagonally in different grain lines (Fig. 7-12C). Have someone holding an iron block or heavy hammer behind the rail as you nail into it in order to take the rebound and get tighter nails.

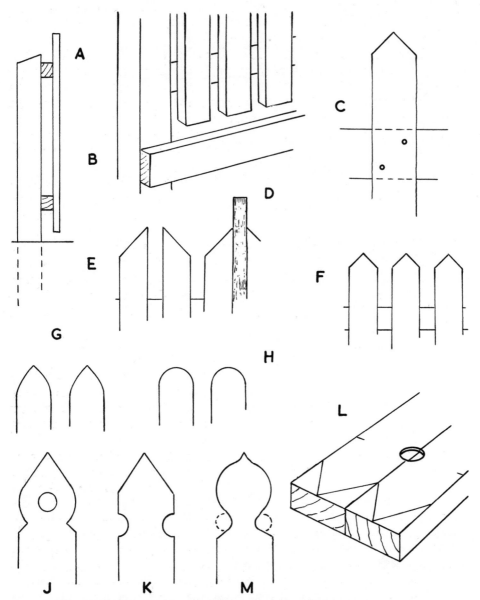

Fig. 7-12. Pickets should be evenly spaced and can have decorated tops.

10. Make sure one picket piece is upright (a post can be your guide). Use a strip of wood as a gauge to keep spacing even (Fig. 7-12D) while working from this first picket. Check squareness and spacing occasionally in case any error is developing.

11. The simplest pickets have square tops. Next simplest is a slope cut one way. Pickets can be nailed on alternate ways (Fig. 7-12E), or a series arranged one way, and then a similar number the other way. More common are simple

points (Fig. 7-12F). Any slope is worth having because it sheds rainwater instead of letting it settle and soak into end grain.

12. Picket tops could go to rounded points or be fully semicircular (Fig. 7-12G and H). If the posts are in line with the pickets, they ought to have matching shapes. That will limit your choice of top design. Another consideration is the number of pickets. A complicated design might appeal to you and be interesting to cut on one picket, but will you feel the same if there are 50 to cut? Use a template to mark tops so they are the same. If you have a bandsaw, the ends are easily shaped; most will have to be cut individually. Cutting two or three in a pile will probably result in noticeable variations.

13. Drilling can be used. There can be a hole through inside a curved outline (Fig. 7-12J). Holes can also be used for edge decoration (Fig. 7-12K). A Forstner bit will make a half hole, but you can use a drill press to go through pickets held together (Fig. 7-12L). A development of this is a gingerbread pattern, with a pair of holes drilled and the bandsaw used to cut into them (Fig. 7-12M).

14. Avoid very sharp upward edges to prevent catching in clothing or scratching skin. If the design includes a point, round it with a file or abrasive. Although sawn shapes are satisfactory, remove raggedness and take off sharpness with a plane or abrasive. It helps to lightly plane off the sharpness of the straight edges of pickets before fixing them.

PRIVACY AND SHELTER FENCES

If you want to hide the view from outside, the fence has to be high and fairly solid. There are some plants that need shelter from the wind and some prefer shade to sunlight. Others flourish so prolifically that they would spread through any open fence. In these situations you need a closed fence, but not necessarily as high as when privacy is the main concern.

Open fences of most types are attractive to look at. A closed fence looks rather plain. You can break up its outline with higher posts or shaped tops, but its barrenness is best broken up by the plants growing in front of it or maybe climbing on it.

A simple solid fence can be made with exterior-grade plywood, this needs rails on posts. If the posts are at 8-foot centers, you can use standard sheets. A height of 4 feet might be all you need for a windbreak, but if you want to go up to 6 feet for privacy there will have to be a joint on a rail. A suitable arrangement would be posts 4 inches or more square, with rails 2 inches square nailed on to support the edges and center of each sheet (Fig. 7-13A). Where sheets join to make up the height, you will be able to nail to a 2 inch rail, but it will be better to have a wider joint rail. With the stiffness of ½-inch plywood helping the rails, supports only at the ends of each panel should be enough. If the result seems to be too flexible, there could be light uprights midway between the posts. Put a capping on the top edge to improve appearance and to prevent water entering the end grain of the plywood. This could be a flat piece, but a shaped strip looks better (Fig. 7-13B).

A closed fence could be made with boards nailed close together (Fig. 7-13C), but plain boards tend to warp. Tongues and grooves at the edges would prevent this (Fig. 7-13D), or you could put battens across at intervals between posts (Fig. 7-13E).

A closed fence could be made by arranging the boards vertically instead of plywood on rails (Fig. 7-13F). Boards nailed over rails at 24-inch intervals will

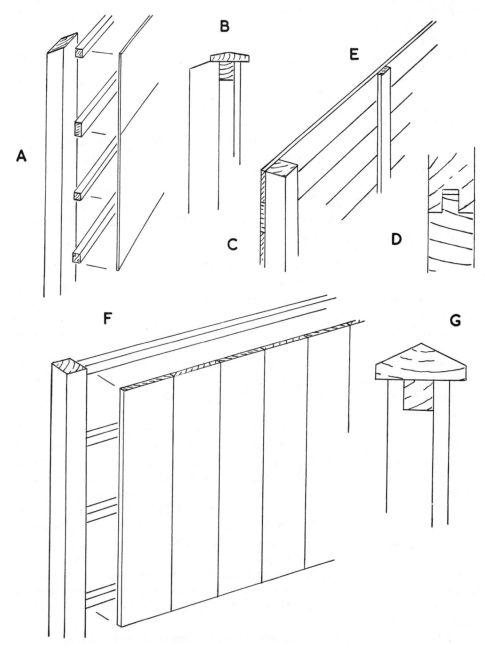

Fig. 7-13. A fence without gaps provides privacy and shelter.

be less likely to warp than those laid horizontally. Use a capping to keep water out of the end grain (Fig. 7-13G).

OPEN BOARDED FENCES

One problem with an expanse of high solid fence is windage. A high wind can put a considerable strain on such a fence, and thus will find the weakest spots and cause breakages. There are ways of making fences that provide privacy and reduction of wind on delicate plants, but when some air is allowed through, the loads on the fence are reduced.

Boards can be arranged on opposite sides of a fence, either horizontally or vertically, to make it difficult for anyone to see through. This also provides good circulation of air (Fig. 7-14).

A picket fence could be made in this way. An existing one might be modified with another row of pickets on the opposite sides of the rails over the gaps (Fig. 7-15A). This could contain spreading plants within bounds or act as a windbreak.

With boards, the simplest arrangement has them horizontal and nailed alternately on opposite sides of the posts (Fig. 7-15B). That might be all that is needed. If the boards seem likely to flex in their length, one or more uprights—of the same thickness as the posts—can be included (Fig. 7-15C). They need not extend above or below the boards. A capping board is not essential, but it will improve appearance and could be just over the upper board or taken the full width (Fig. 7-15D).

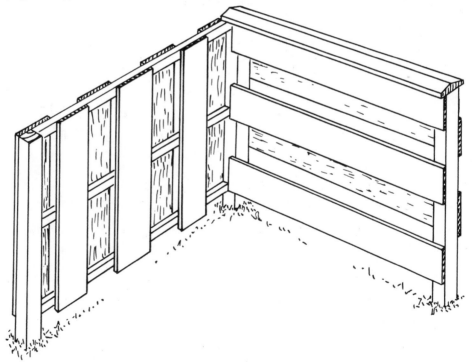

Fig. 7-14. A fence with boards on opposite sides lets air through, but provides privacy.

There are several ways of supporting vertical boards on opposite sides of a fence so they alternate and obscure the view without stopping air. If the boards are to come outside the lines of the posts, the rails should be as thick as the posts. They might be tenoned into the posts, but it is easier to use spacers and nail to them (Fig. 7-15E). For a fence about 6 feet high, there should be rails at top and bottom of the boards and two intermediate ones.

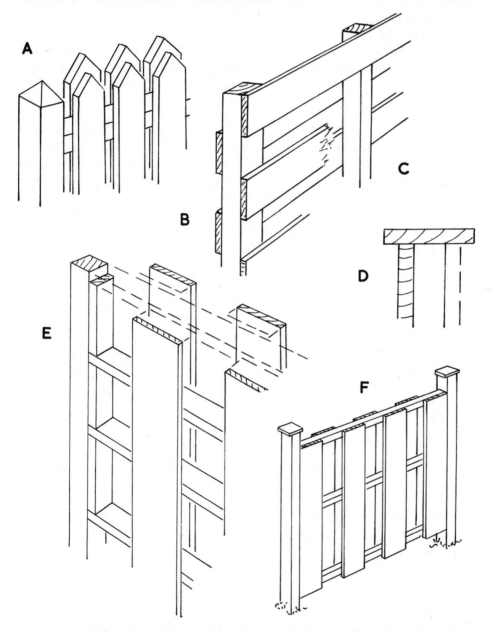

Fig. 7-15. Boards can be upright or horizontal in an open boarded fence.

In that type of fence, carry the boards over the posts so that you can space them along a fence with many posts without having to fit into post spacing. Arrange capping boards to overhang the tops a little.

Alternatively, arrange the boards between and level with the surfaces of the posts, that allows you to break up plainness by taking the posts higher (Fig. 7-15F). The rails could be fitted with tapered ends into mortises, as described for earlier fences, but it will be simpler to use the same method as the previous example—with the rails narrowed.

If the posts are 4 inches thick and the boards are 1 inch, that means rails 2 inches thick. They could be deeper for stiffness. If the posts are not too far apart, 2-inch-square rails should be adequate. Nail the rails to spacers, and then the boards will fit level with the posts. The tops of the posts could be cut level and a capping board continued over them, or you can take each post higher and shape its top or give it its own capping.

Another way to use vertical boards to let air through and provide partial privacy is to set them diagonal to make louvers (Fig. 7-16). You cannot provide intermediate stiffening. The boards should be selected for their straightness of grain. Warped boards would spoil the appearance, if not the effect, of such a fence.

Fig. 7-16. Fence boards set at an angle will let air through and provide some privacy.

The angle used for the boards affects the degree of privacy. You could put 6-inch boards at 45 degrees with their edges opposite (Fig. 7-17A). This means that anyone looking through can get a fairly complete view at that angle as the gaps are fairly wide. If you want to reduce the view, the boards can be placed at a more acute angle to the line of the fence (Fig. 7-17B). The boards can also be arranged to overlap instead of having their edges opposite (Fig. 7-17C).

If the boards are arranged more acutely and their edges are to overlap, the spacers become narrower. They also need narrower rail surfaces (compare Fig. 7-17A and B). For these two examples, the rails could be 2 × 4s, with the 4-inch-width horizontal for a 45-degree angle or the 2-inch surface horizontal for a 30-degree angle. Leave small gaps at the posts or bring the boards close if you want to obstruct any view through there.

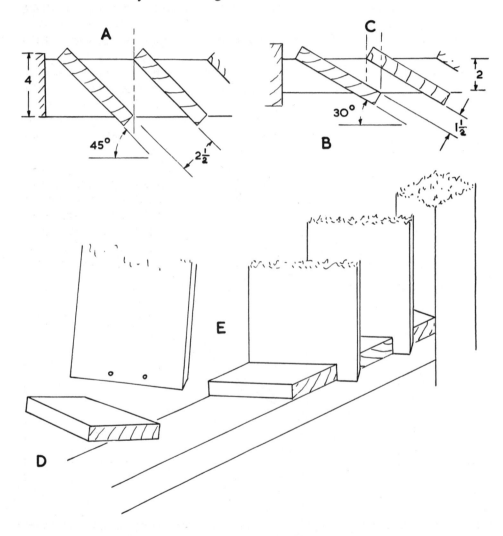

Fig. 7-17. Boards mounted at an angle are set between blocks.

Make the spacers thick enough to take nails securely (1 ½ inch deep should be enough). Draw a full-size section of fence, and from this get the sizes and shapes of the spacers (Fig. 7-17D) so you can make as many as you need before you start assembling the fence. There will have to be square-edged pieces against the posts. If you start assembly from one post, you can nail a board to a spacer before placing the next one (Fig. 7-17E).

GATES

A gate should close properly in its opening, swing far enough open, and keep its shape. In many gardens, the gateposts move, the gate distorts, and passage through a fence becomes a frustrating and disappointing performance. This indicates that more thought should be given to gate design and construction than is often considered. Most garden gates do not have to open more than is needed to push a barrow through. For the usual pedestrian passage, a width of 30 inches should do.

The pair of gateposts should be rigid, upright, and usually of a larger section than the ordinary fence posts. In particular, the one on the hinge side of the gate should be immovable. If possible, sight across the two posts to see that they are parallel in that direction. Of course, they should also be parallel in the direction the gate has to fit. You cannot make a good job of hanging a gate if there are faults in the gateposts.

A gate is supported by its hinges on one side and it has to be designed so it does not drop out of shape. If it is faced completely with plywood that will hold it in shape. If it is built up of pieces, they must be braced properly. If there is a piece put diagonally across an assembly of boards and it slopes down from the hinged side (Fig. 7-18A), it is in tension. If it slopes up, it is in compression (Fig. 7-18B). Because it is easier to make a small gate with a strut effective in compression, that is the usual way. Some large gates have diagonals in tension, but then loads have to be taken via bolts.

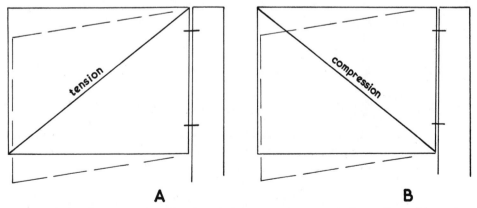

Fig. 7-18. When designing a framed gate, resistance to sagging can come from a diagonal in tension or one in compression.

WICKET GATE

The most frequent need is for a gate in a fence to be at waist height. It might be a picket fence and the pattern of the fence could be carried on to the gate. Elsewhere there could be vertical boards that are perhaps wider than those to match pickets. In general, the wider and fewer boards in a gate the less the risk of it falling out of shape. Figure 7-19 shows a satisfactory method of making a small gate that can be adapted to those of other sizes. It has a straight top, but boards can be shaped to match pickets.

The wood for a gate can be the same as for the fence. If you have used partially seasoned wood for the fence, it would be better to select fully seasoned wood for the gate in order to reduce the risk of warping, shrinking, and splitting. Gates are sometimes made of very light wood, but anything less than ¾ inch thick is inadvisable. This gate should be all 1-inch (⅞-inch-planed) wood.

Fig. 7-19. A wicket gate makes a pedestrian entrance through a fence.

Materials List for Wicket Gate

7 uprights	35	×	4	×	1
2 crosspieces	30	×	4	×	1
1 diagonal	36	×	4	×	1
1 cap	30	×	2½	×	1

Unless there is a particular need for a closed-panel gate, it is advisable to make the gate with gaps between the boards. This allows for expansion and contraction with little effect on the overall width.

1. Prepare the boards for the upright parts. See that the edges are straight. Mark the lengths, but you can leave cutting the tops until after the crosspiece has been fitted.

2. Mark the positions of the two crosspieces (Fig. 7-20A). Make the crosspieces and mark on them the positions of the uprights (Fig. 7-20B), which will be evenly spaced. With these markings as a guide, drill the crosspieces for

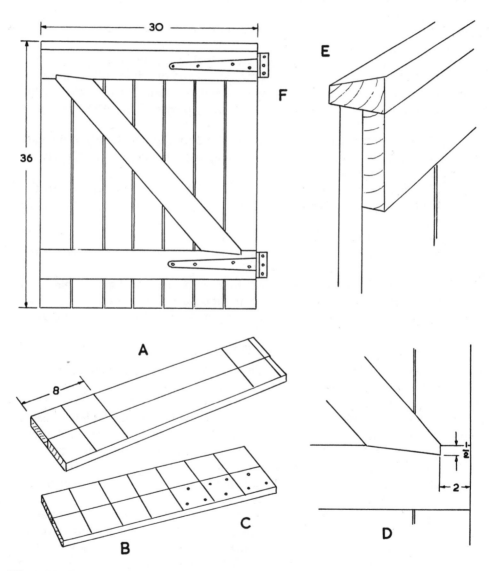

Fig. 7-20. Constructional details of the wicket gate.

screws. Three or four screws at each crossing are advisable (Fig. 7-20C). Although the gate might be nailed, screwed construction will be stronger.

3. Put the outside uprights and the crosspieces together face down on a flat surface. Check squareness and join them with one temporary screw at each crossing.

4. Lay the wood for the diagonal strut across and mark on it the line of the crosspieces. Mark on the crosspieces where it comes (Fig. 7-21A). The strut could be cut across on this line to fit close to the other parts, but the greatest resistance to gate distortion comes from notching it in. With the lines drawn as a guide, mark and cut the shaped ends (Fig. 7-20C).

5. Put the strut in place and from it mark on the crosspieces what has to be cut out (Fig. 7-21B). This should be a tight fit. Cut inside the lines after taking the assembly apart.

6. Re-assemble the four pieces and check that the shape is correct when the strut is in position. Fully screw these corner joints and put in the other uprights. Fit in the strut and screw it where it crosses the other parts. There could be glue in the notches, but the gate should be satisfactory if assembled dry with screws only.

7. Trim the tops of the boards and add the capping (Fig. 7-20E). If the gate is to swing back flat against a wall or fence, keep the inner edge level. Otherwise a small overlap can be allowed.

8. T-hinges are most appropriate, but other types could be used. Put the hinges on the crosspieces (Fig. 7-20F) and on to the gatepost (with a little clearance).

9. At the other side, put a stop strip on the post (Fig. 7-21C). This could get some rough treatment, and 1-inch-square hardwood is suitable even if the gate has been made of softwood.

10. There are several types of catches that can be used on a garden gate, but a strip of hardwood used as a turnbutton might be all that is needed (Fig. 7-21D). Put washers under the screw head and between the turnbutton and the post.

TALL GATE

If a fence is high and intended to provide privacy or act as a windbreak, any gate in it ought to also be high. This means having tall gateposts with a greater risk of the gate fitting badly later if they move only slightly. A move is more likely at the greater height unless the posts can be restrained. Fortunately, it is possible to put a piece across above head height so that the posts are braced to each other and held parallel (Fig. 7-22). This depends on the fence height, but if you can take the posts to 6 feet 6 inches or more you can make a rigid gateway. The ranch-style piece across could have shallow notches to fit over the posts. Something more than nails will be resisting movement.

The gate can be made in a similar way to the previous one, but there are a few points to note when working to a greater height. This gate is shown made of boards 6 inches wide and 1 inch thick (Fig. 7-23A). The top is shown cut to a curve, but it could be made straight across with a capping if you prefer. The

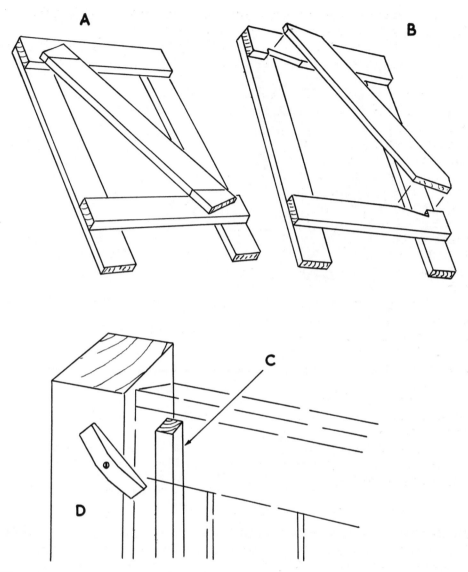

Fig. 7-21. Arrangements of the brace, stop, and catch.

three crosspieces (*ledgers*) are necessary, but the middle one is better not exactly midway between the other two. If it is central, an optical illusion makes it look lower. (You might decide that does not matter.) You cannot reach over to a fastener—as you can with the previous gate—so the latch or lock has to be workable from either side.

    1. Set out the door and assemble the outside boards with the crosspieces each held with single screws. Have this square and position the diagonals so that you can mark their ends and the notches in the same way as described for the previous door. Because of the different spacings, the diagonals will be at different

Fig. 7-22. A tall gate in a high fence
is best with a piece over the
opening.

Materials List for Tall Gate					
5 uprights	72	×	6	×	1
2 crosspieces	30	×	6	×	1
2 diagonals	34	×	6	×	1
2 handles	15	×	3	×	1¼
1 latch	15	×	1½	×	¾
latches from	12	×	2	×	1¼

angles. If you want to keep the slopes the same, you can position one and arrange
the other so it is at the same angle, letting its ends come as they will on the
crosspieces.

2. The curve of the top is best left for marking and cutting until after the
door is assembled, but you can make the ends approximately to shape. This is
particularly appropriate if you want to use up short boards at the outsides.

3. Assemble the door with all the boards equally spaced. Planed wood will
leave gaps up to ¼ inch between edges.

4. Improvise a compass with a strip of wood, an awl, and a pencil (Fig.
7-23B). The curve drawn is 30 inch radius, but you can vary this if a flatter or
greater curve would look better for your gate. Cut the top and take off any
sharpness of the edges.

5. Fit a hinge central on each crosspiece. T-hinges 12 inches long would be
a good choice. Hang the gate temporarily with one screw in each hinge and check

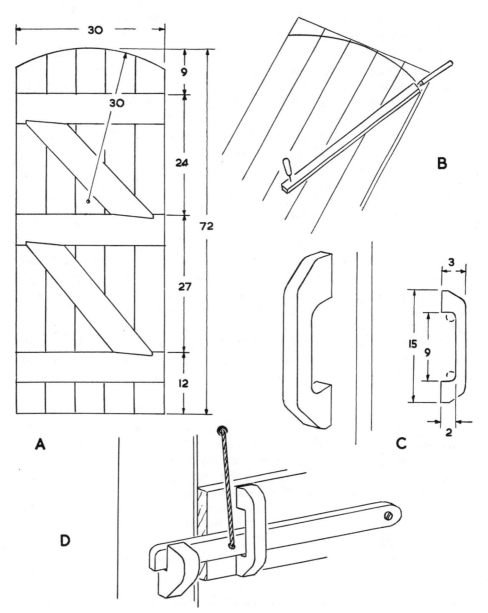

Fig. 7-23. Suggested sizes and details of a tall gate.

its action. Position a stop to let the gate shut with the ledgers level with the post surface.

6. You could use purchased metal handles on each side of the gate and a latch of the type that allows opening from either side. If it is an outside fence, you might want to fit a lock or there could be bolts on the inside. Alternatively, you can make handles and latch.

7. Even if the gate is made of softwood, the handles and latches should be close-grained hardwood for strength and resistance to wear.

8. The handles are about 1¼ inch thick. Mark out (Fig. 7-23C), and drill the corners of the openings and cut the shape. Make sure the parts that come against the door are kept flat, but all the other edges and corners should be thoroughly rounded. Fit the handles at suitable heights by screwing through the door into them. Stagger them slightly so you can drive screws from both sides.

9. The latch is a strip of wood loosely pivoted on a screw, with washers under the head and between it and the door. Heavy hardwood about 1½ inches wide, ¾ inch thick, and 15 inches long would be about right. Within reason length is an advantage. This drops into a notched block on the post (Fig. 7-23D). The block is made like part of a handle. The bottom of the notch comes opposite the latch strip when it is level. Give its front a rounded slope so the strip will slide into it and drop in when the gate is shut.

On the door, there is a retaining piece over the latch strip. Get its size from the latch temporarily assembled. The bottom edge of the opening should come below the strip when it rests in the bottom of the block on the post. The top edge of the opening should allow the strip to lift clear of the notch. For raising the latch from the other side, use a cord through a hole in the strip and a loosely fitting hole in the door.

Counterbore the hole in the strip so the knot can pull in. Have a loop or large knot in the other end of the cord so it can be gripped and will not pull back through the hole in the door.

PLYWOOD GATE

Modern synthetic resin waterproof glues have such a good resistance to moisture that it is possible to use plywood made with them and structures assembled with them outdoors with confidence. The only possible problem with plywood marked "exterior" or "marine" is that water might enter the edges of the veneers and cause them to swell or rot. Edges should be protected. If this is done, a gate can be faced with suitable plywood and used in a fence or elsewhere outdoors.

This project is a small gate (Fig. 7-24), but the same method could be used for a pair of gates or a larger one. The two faces are plywood. Framing inside strengthens it and provides solid places where attachments come. There is a

Materials List for Plywood Gate						
2 panels	39	×	29	×	½	plywood
2 sides	39	×	3	×	1	
1 bottom	29	×	3	×	1	
1 center rail	23	×	3	×	1	
1 top	23	×	4	×	1	
2 lips	38	×	2¼	×	⅜	
2 lips	34	×	2¼	×	⅜	

Fig. 7-24. A flush paneled gate can be covered with plywood.

lipping around top and sides where rainwater might otherwise enter. If the bottom is expected to get wet, that could be lipped as well.

The faces are exterior- or marine-grade plywood ½ inch or less thickness. The internal parts can be softwood. The lips can be hardwood or softwood and could be chosen to match the appearance of the plywood if there is to be a clear varnish finish.

1. Set out the size and shape of the door on one piece of plywood (Fig. 7-25A). The top could be straight, but it is shown with a slight curve. Avoid much curve because there might be difficulty in making the lip conform and stay in place. Cut the plywood to size and check that it suits the gateway, if that has already been prepared.

2. Cut the pieces that will form the internal framing. They suit the outline, and one piece across the center should provide all the stiffness needed on a gate of this size (Fig. 7-25B). If you intend using a handle, lock, or catch that would be wider than the framing, have a block inside (Fig. 7-25C) to take any screws or holes. Ordinary hinges will probably come within the framing, but if you are using T-hinges place pieces to take their long arms (Fig. 7-25D).

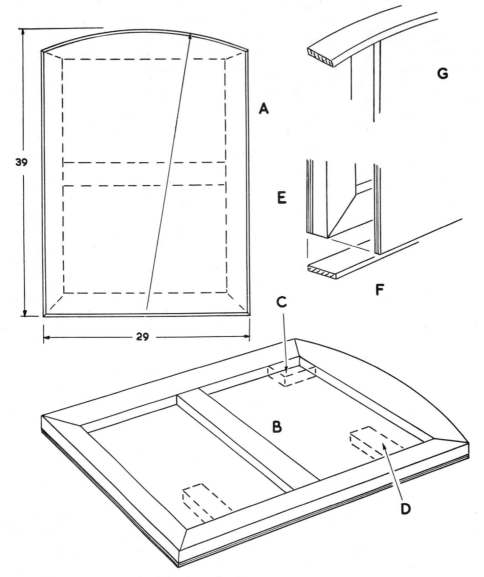

Fig. 7-25. Sizes and details of the plywood gate.

3. Glue does not hold so well on end grain. Avoid it at the corners by mitering the frames (Fig. 7-25E). Expose side grain only to the lips.

4. Glue the framing to the plywood. Locate and secure it, while the glue sets, with nails through the plywood. There should be no need for screws providing the parts are kept in close contact. Clamps or weights can be used.

5. Level the framing surfaces if necessary. Cut the other plywood panel slightly oversize. Glue and nail it on, with clamps or weights, until the glue has set. Then trim the edges all round.

6. Prepare the material for the lips slightly too wide so that is can be planed level after attaching. It would be unwise to make it only just wide enough because planing the plywood surfaces should be avoided. That might be necessary if you found the lip edge slightly narrower than the plywood.

7. If there is to be a lip at the bottom, fix that first. Use plenty of glue so that the plywood is sealed. Use nails to hold the lip in place. Trim its ends to match the framing (Fig. 7-25F).

8. The lips at the sides and top are attached in the same way, but the top has to be pulled to the curve. It helps in doing that if the side lips are trimmed to the curve and the top piece is allowed to overhang a few inches at first (Fig. 7-25G). That allows you to put on pressure over the corners, where there is the greatest risk of the joint opening. Trim the ends after the glue has set. Many of these glues build up strength over several days, after they have apparently set, so delay trimming and planing edges of lips level for this period.

9. Completion of the gate involves the attachment of hinges and fastener, in a similar way to previous projects. Thorough painting is usually the best finish for this type of gate. The solid face of the gate is a good place for the name or number of your home. If that is painted on, there is no need for advance preparation. If you intend to screw on numbers or a nameplate, arrange a block inside to take the screws.

8
CHAPTER

Decks
and Walkways

If you live in an area where the climate is suitable, one of the best ways of providing a suitable outside living area is to make a deck. A wood deck is attractive and less costly than providing a stone, concrete, or other hard surface deck or patio. If the ground is uneven or has a considerable slope, a wood deck on posts might be the only feasible way of making an outdoor extension to your home. It should be large enough for many chairs and tables, barbeque, and all the other things that make for comfortable outdoor living.

If part of your property is very uneven or "swampy," you might want to make a raised walkway for convenient access to another part of the garden. In general, the making of a walkway is similar to a deck. Posts and beams have to be provided in a similar way, and there will almost certainly have to be handrails. All are constructed in a way similar to parts of a deck. A shorter walkway would be better described as a bridge, possibly over a ditch. If it is on posts, rather than cantilevered out from the banks, it is made in a very similar way. You might want to make a walkway, around your home, where the ground is uneven and a level path is required. That could be treated as a deck even though it may be narrower and simpler.

Obviously, you need to a design and build to suit the situation. Broadly, they are divided into low-level and high-level decks. A low-level deck extends, usually from your house, over ground that might be slightly uneven. Perhaps at the edge it is no more than a step down to the surrounding ground. There is usually no need for protection around it.

A high-level deck might start high and continue over ground that is at a slope. It would have fairly high posts at its extremity. It could start at the ground and continue level although the ground below slopes away. In these cases, there has to be protection to prevent users from falling off and there will have to be stairs if you want an outside connection with the ground. In some places, a deck can be classed as low level for much of its area, and then it extends over sloping ground as a high-level deck to give you valuable outdoor living space where there was none before.

It is usual for the boards of a deck to have narrow gaps between. In most circumstances, this is a good arrangement as rainwater and dirt will fall through and the deck is easily kept clean. The deck might require a closed, solid surface as when it is over a working or living area that has to be protected. Then the boards can be laid close and caulked. The top edges must be prepared with bevels to take this.

Alternatively, plywood could be laid with joints close fitting and glued or caulked. Besides the plywood being exterior or marine grade, it is advisable to coat the surface with one of the mastic treatments that leaves a thick, hard-wearing waterproof skin. General construction for a close-fitting deck is the same as for the more usual open type.

The surface of a deck with narrow gaps can be formed with boards that are wider than they are deep (Fig. 8-1A) or by deeper boards standing on edge (Fig. 8-1B). The second type of deck is more costly because more wood is used, but

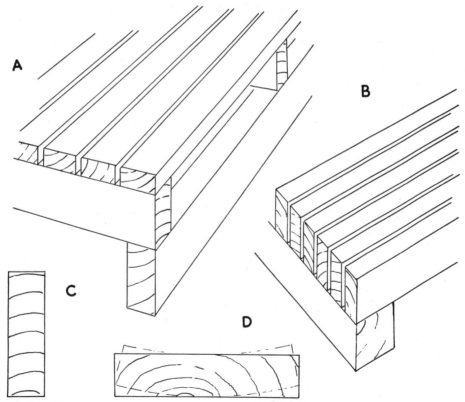

Fig. 8-1. The arrangement of parts of a deck. The probable direction of warping as seen from the grain lines.

less wood is needed for other parts in the supporting framing. The edgewise boards have greater stiffness and do not need as much stiffening below.

In the usual construction of a raised deck, the deck boards are supported on joists that are edgewise and close enough together to give rigidity to the walking surface. These, in turn, are held up by beams that are larger in section and also edgewise. They are attached to the posts connected with the ground. If there is a railing around the deck, its supporting posts are bolted to the beams or joists (Fig. 8-2). When the deck boards are deeper than they are wide, the joists can be wider apart and there may be no need for beams in a low deck.

Although there are parts of a deck assembly where strips could be notched together or mortise and tenon joints used, it is more common to rely on nails, lag screws, and bolts. The parts merely overlap or rest on one another. Sections of wood are not then reduced so strength is maintained. If greater strength is required, joints can be reinforced with metal angle brackets, and there are special metal straps and supports available to suit standard wood sections. Cutting away wood is then only done if necessary to bring surfaces level.

Lumber with a good resistance to exposure to all kinds of weather is needed. The ideal wood might not be available, but a deck should be expected to have a long life with little attention. Much depends on the wood from which it is made. You will have to depend on local availability. The wood should have a natural

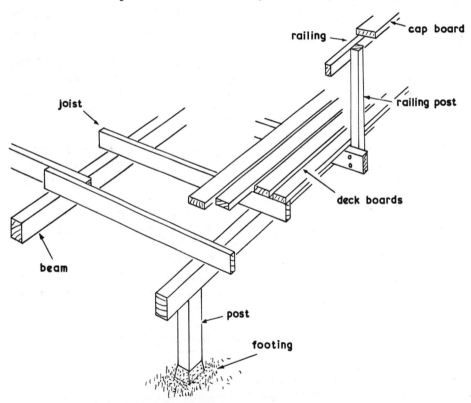

Fig. 8-2. The names of the main parts of a deck.

resistance to rot, but it can also be treated with preservative. It should have strength and stiffness, and its surface should wear well and have little tendency to splinter. Whatever the wood chosen, it is better if it is heartwood (cut from near the center of the tree). Sapwood (from nearer the bark) is inferior in all properties.

You will have to consider shrinking and warping. If a board is cut radially from the log, the grain lines are across and the effect of taking up or releasing moisture will be on the thickness and have negligible effect on the other direction (Fig. 8-1C). This means edgewise deck boards would not vary on the surface (whether wet or dry). If the wood is cut elsewhere from the log, the grain lines will show curves completely or partially toward one side (Fig. 8-1D). If the wood takes up moisture it will warp outward. Think of it as the grain lines trying to straighten. Deck boards are better laid with the outer bark side of the wood upward so that warping causes the edges to lift. This is less of a problem than having the center of the board try to lift. The edges can be leveled by planing or power sanding.

Some woods that have been found suitable for decks are Douglas fir, western larch, southern pine, redwood, cedar, cypress, and white oak. The man at the local lumberyard should be able to suggest which of his stock should suit your needs.

A simple inconspicuous deck might be your concern. If your plans are more ambitious, it will be wise to check that what you are doing conforms to building codes or planning ordinances before starting work.

The instructions that follow are for typical deck constructions. Every individual situation will have its own problems of design and techniques, but these examples will provide guidance and show possible ways of getting the results you want.

LOW-LEVEL EDGE BOARD DECK

Figure 8-3 shows an example of a deck, not far above ground level, with the main area made with boards on edge. It is assumed that the deck will be about 7 feet from back to front and 10 feet wide. The ground does not have to be level, but variations should not be very great.

The suggested deck boards are 2 inches wide and 4 inches deep, with the supporting joists 4 inches square. Over most types of grade or soil, it should be sufficient to provide nine supporting footings. If the rear of the deck is against a house, it might be possible to get support there without the need for footings.

1. Survey the area the deck will cover. Because the deck will be too close to the ground for maintenance after it is finished, clear away rubbish, remove

Materials List for Low-Level Edge Board Deck	
3 joists	120 × 4 × 4
54 deck boards	84 × 4 × 2

Fig. 8-3. Layout of a low-level edge board deck.

large stones, and treat the area with weed killer. Excessive unevenness can be leveled.

2. Check levels. If the deck will be against a wall, you will know where you want its surface to be. Mark on the wall where the undersides of the joists will be to achieve this level or put a temporary board there (Fig. 8-4A). From this line, use a long, straight board and a spirit level to check where the heights will be at the limits of the deck (Fig. 8-4B). Drive temporary pegs to mark the heights at these points. Check in the other direction that the peg tops are level, this will show you if what you want to do is feasible on the land. If there are high spots where joists would have to go below ground level, you must remove soil because the wood must have at least a few inches clearance.

3. Leave the temporary pegs in place for future reference, but now—working square to the wall—mark where the lines of the joists will come and where three supports for each will be. At each of these points, there will have to be footings (Fig. 8-4C).

4. In the simplest construction, the supports can be short posts driven into the ground. With suitably treated wood of the right type, this will give a life of many years. Unlike a fence post that can be replaced or repaired fairly easily, a rotted support under a low deck is almost impossible to attend to without major work. It is better to use only concrete. If the ground falls away and you have to use a post anywhere, that should be arranged as described in the next project. If variations of height are not much, concrete supports can be made to the same height despite differences in grade level.

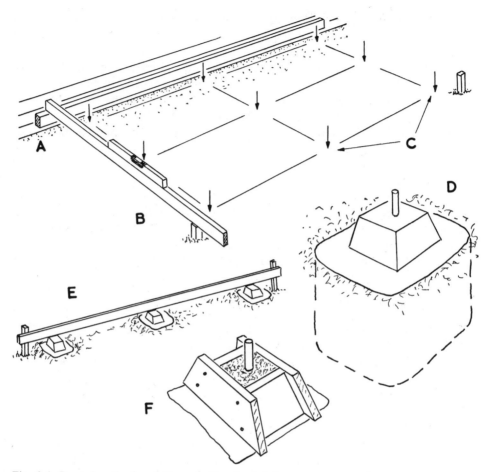

Fig. 8-4. Preparing the foundations of a low-level deck.

5. For concrete footings, dig holes to be filled with concrete. How big and how deep depends on the soil. Loose, sandy soil will need a greater spread than heavy clay. A typical hole will be about 12 inches in each direction.

6. Although the concrete in the ground will cover whatever area is necessary to provide support, the part that comes against the joist should be no wider than the joist (in this case 4 inches) and arranged to slope away (Fig. 8-4D). There should be a steel rod or bolt projecting to fit in a hole in the joist and locate it.

7. The support does not have to be made with the precision that would be needed when casting a concrete container or ornament that would be visible, but when you start concrete work have wood ready to make forms to give shape to these parts. The concrete in the holes can all be poured and well tamped down. Leave it until it begins to harden before adding the above-ground parts. There could be a few long nails or metal rods pushed in where the supports will come to bond the two lots of concrete together.

8. At each line of supports, use a straight piece of wood on stakes driven into the ground to indicate the height and where one edge of the top has to be (Fig. 8-4E).

9. Make up simple forms for each place to the correct height and pour in concrete. Have an iron rod set in the top and projecting about 2 inches (Fig. 8-4F).

10. Leave all this for the concrete to harden enough for the forms to be removed. Leave a few more days for it to cure fully.

11. Make the joists. Drill overdepth for the pegs on the supports. Either cut the ends now or leave them until after the decking has been fitted. A slope back encourages water to run off and not soak into the end grain (Fig. 8-5A). Treat the joists with preservative.

12. At each support, make a pad of roofing paper and waterproof mastic so the wood will bed down on that (Fig. 8-5B). If possible, fit all three joists during one working session. It is unlikely that you will achieve perfect level between them. Use your long straightedge and spirit level along the joists (across them and diagonally). You can get a good level by cutting away the wood where it

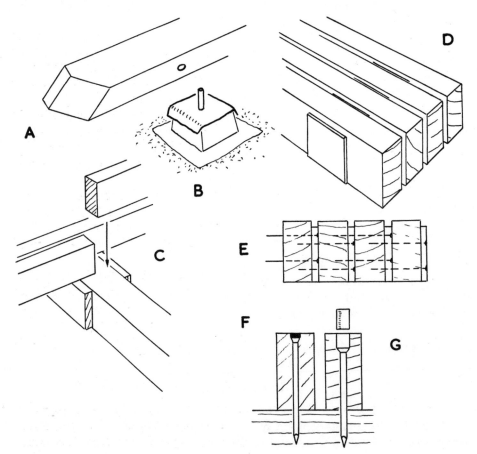

Fig. 8-5. Constructional details of a low-level decks.

rests on one support, but you are more likely to need to pack up to bring joists up to the highest point you discover. More roofing paper and mastic might be all that is needed. You might need wood packings, but make sure the whole support area is covered and everything you add is made waterproof with mastic. Press and hammer the joists tight. You do not want them settling further in use. Finally, if there is space, get back and sight across all joists to see that they are really level and parallel. A twist in a deck is something to be avoided.

13. The foregoing instructions assume the deck is to be level. It could be given a slight slope so water drains away from the house and does not settle on the deck. That might seem a good idea, but you cannot provide much slope without it becoming noticeable, and only a slight slope is not very effective. If you want to provide a slope, use the leveling board with a packing under its end to arrive at the level at the outer edge. A drop of 2 inches in the 7 foot length is as much as might be provided without the angle becoming apparent.

14. In a deck of the size suggested, deck boards will almost certainly be full length. There can be an occasional joint on the middle joist if you want to use up short pieces. However, the joist should be thickened with cleats nailed on to provide support under the joint (Fig. 8-5C). Short boards should not come more often than every fifth piece laid.

15. The deck boards should have gaps between ⅛ inch and ¼ inch. To maintain that, prepare spacers that can come over the joists. These could be pieces of shingle, tempered hardboard, or strips cut specially. Have the grain the same way as the deck boards. Square pieces cut to come ½ inch below the top level will do (Fig. 8-5D).

16. The deck boards can be nailed through the spacers into each other in groups of a size you can handle; four at a time will probably be enough. Stagger the nails and leave the points projecting to go into a batch already mounted (Fig. 8-5E). The boards should have been treated with preservative, but as you assemble with the spacers also coat the joints with a waterproof mastic.

17. Predrill for nails into the joists to reduce the risk of splitting. Nails can be punched below the surface and covered with stopping (Fig. 8-5F), or they can be counterbored so they are deep enough for covering with a wood plug (Fig. 8-5G). As you fit each board or prepared batch, cover the joist with waterproof mastic or roofing paper or felt.

18. Nailing batches of boards together first will ensure that they finish upright, but where you fit single boards check that the ends are standing upright. Make sure the exposed ends of boards are level. Clean off any raggedness from sawing. If you make intermediate joints, the two pieces need not butt together tightly. The joist will not usually extend past the outside deck boards. If they are cut level and slope back, they should not suffer from water penetration.

HIGH DECK

If your home is on a hillside or you want to make a deck higher than ground level, it has to be supported on posts for at least part of the area. Much depends on the actual situation, but this deck is 20 feet long and extending 8 feet from the house wall. Its inner edge is supported on the house side a short distance above the ground, and the further edge is supported on posts arranged to suit variations in the sloping ground (Fig. 8-6). The surface is made of 2-inch-by-4-inch boards laid flat on joists that are supported at their outer ends on a beam with posts. There is a railing all round. One possible stair arrangement is suggested in the next project.

In this arrangement, the beam is joined midway over a post and the gap between post centers is 60 inches. The joists on this are 24 inches apart, and they

Materials List for High Deck

(length to suit situation)

posts	4 × 4
beams	8 × 4
joists	8 × 2
deck boards	4 × 2
railing posts	3 × 3
rails	4 × 2
capping	6 × 2

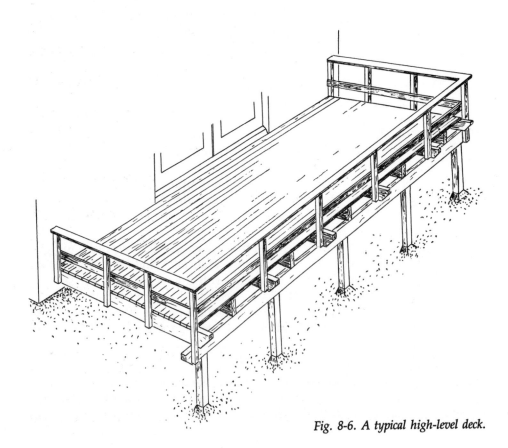

Fig. 8-6. A typical high-level deck.

can span the distance to the house side without intermediate supports. If your arrangement involves spacing the posts more than 60 inches apart, the beam depth should be increased. The joist spands should not be increased very much unless they are deepened. It is assumed that the 4-inch-square posts will not have to be more than 60 inches high. A larger section should be used for higher posts.

Treat the wood in the way described in the previous project (with preservative and waterproof felt or paper in joists). If any metal is not rustproofed, use a rust-inhibiting fluid on steel and protect it with paint.

The actual fitting of deck boards is to joists and joists to beams. The adding of a railing is all straightforward, but there are some other details of construction that should be settled before starting work. In particular, you need to know how the deck will be attached to the house side.

1. With the deck boards laid parallel to the house side, the ends of the joists will come to the side and have to be supported there. The strength of the house structure must be checked. Usually there are strong members that will take lag screws or other fasteners through the siding or other covering. The locations of nails will give you a clue to positions. It may be possible to fix a ledger along the side and have the joist ends rest on it (Fig. 8-7A). If that is securely fastened it should take the weight. To prevent the joists from pulling away from the house, there could be a steel bracket at each joist or you could use a long piece of steel angle (Fig. 8-7B) with screws upward into the joists.

2. If it is inconvenient to use a ledger or your need to spread the fasteners, a board of a similar section to the joist can be attached to the house. The joist ends are then held by metal joist hangers (Fig. 8-7C), with screws through both ways.

3. With the house connections decided, it will be a help to make a light assembly of scrap wood to the outline of the deck and with other pieces in the place of the posts to check on positions of footings and the general layout.

4. The footings can be dealt with in a similar way to those of the last project. The projecting bolt or spike goes into the end grain of the post, and a packing of roofing felt and mastic seals the wood.

5. Other ways of mounting the posts, to keep them clear of the ground and the risk of rot, involve steel anchor straps that might have to be made specially. One type uses steel (about 2-inch-by-$\frac{3}{8}$-inch section) forged to a loop that can be set in the concrete. Then the foot of the post is held by bolts between the two arms (Fig. 8-7D).

6. At the beam, the posts are best held with metal connectors. There could be angles with two lag screws each way (Fig. 8-7E). There could be steel strips each side bolted through or with lag screws (Fig. 8-7F). A further step would be to take a strip as a band over the beam (Fig. 8-7G).

7. For a joint over the center post, the two parts would not get much bearing on the post top. The post could be widened with a strip across. A cover piece goes inside and there is a metal strap outside (Fig. 8-7H).

8. The joists on top of the beam can be held down in various ways, but toe nailing is simple (Fig. 8-7J). Drill for the nails to reduce risk of splitting. For

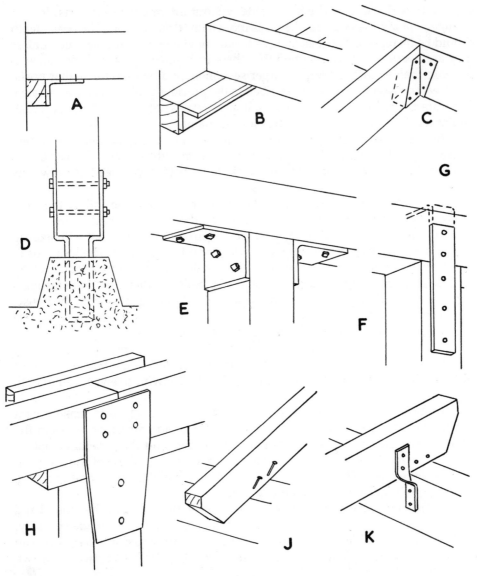

Fig. 8-7. Post and framing arrangements for a high-level deck.

additional strength, particularly where high winds might be expected to produce lifting forces, there can be twisted strip-metal straps (Fig. 8-7K).

9. Plan the deck layout so that alternate joists extend over the beam about 12 inches to take the railing posts. For a stronger railing, allow for posts on every joist. At the ends, let the beam also extend far enough to take railing posts, and have the end joists level with the end of the deck boards so more railing posts can be mounted along them (Fig. 8-8A).

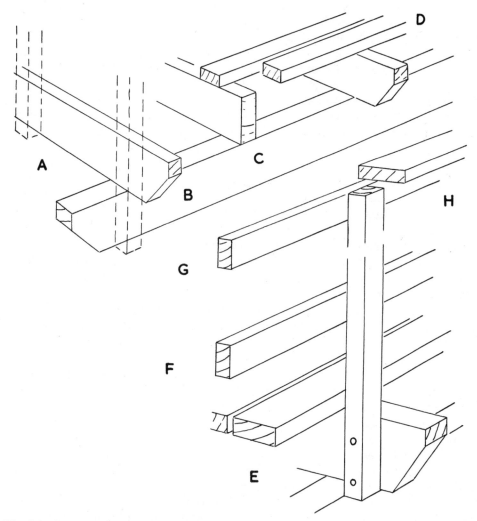

Fig. 8-8. Arrangements for railing posts on a high-level deck.

10. Prepare the posts. Level their tops with each other and check their level in relation to the attachments on the houseside. Mount the beam on the posts. Set them vertically before making the joints. Use temporary struts to the house side and others to the ground, if necessary. Fit the two end joist (Fig. 8-8B). Mark out for other joists at 24-inch intervals (Fig. 8-8C). Fit one near the center next to steady the assembly, and then add the other joists. Check diagonal measurements to see that the assembly is square.

11. Depending on the lengths available, there will have to be joints in the deck boards. Stagger the joints and thicken the joists where they come. You will be able to arrange some joints at the center, and probably have to divide the total length into about thirds.

12. Nail the deck boards with two nails at each crossing. Drill at the ends to reduce risk of splitting, and elsewhere if you wish to counterbore and cover the nail heads with plugs. Lay the outside boards directly over the beam (Fig. 8-8D). Space the others inward from this with boards laid flat, there is no need to include spacers. Use a short length of ¼-inch-thick wood as a gauge as you fit boards alongside those already laid.

13. With the deck boards fitted, the assembly should be rigid. Trim the board ends, if necessary, and remove raggedness from sawing. Check that all joints are tight, this is particularly important for lag screws and bolts.

14. The railing is intended to be 30 inches above the deck boards and have one intermediate rail. It could be arranged like a closed fence (as already described) or the height could be varied. Cut the posts from 3-inch-square wood that is long enough to overlap the joists at the ends and sides. The two longer posts go over the beams at the corners. Bolt the posts to the alternate joist ends (Fig. 8-8E). Check that they are vertical and sight along to see that they are in line. At the corners, put the posts on the outsides of the beams so that they will be in line with the other posts both ways. At the deck ends, bolt the posts to the joists at about 36-inch intervals.

15. In most situations, the lower rail can be inside the posts about 12 inches above the deck (Fig. 8-8F). It could be 2-inch-by-4-inch wood or rather thinner. Make joints on posts as needed. At the corners, one rail could go above the other. Long screws could be used or bolts could be taken through.

16. At the top, there is a similar rail level with the tops of the posts (Fig. 8-8G). A flat capping is put over it (preferably) wide enough to cover the posts and prevent water entering the end grain (Fig. 8-8H). If you cannot cover all of the post, taper the exposed part to encourage water to run off. Miter the capping corners.

17. Trim the ends of the joists and beams, but do not cut back close to the railing posts because that would leave short end grain in line with the bolts. The end grain might break through under pressure.

18. The edges of the capping and rails should be rounded, and any other parts that could come into contact with skin should have sharpeness removed.

19. If the deck is firmly secured by attachment to the house and none of the posts are more than 5 feet high, there should be no fear of unsteadiness or movement due to activities on top or high winds blowing underneath. If stiffening is required due to tall posts, there will have to be some bracing.

20. The most effective bracing comes from diagonal struts from the base of one post to the top of another. They could come inside and outside and be bolted through so that they slope alternate ways (Fig. 8-9A). However, this makes access underneath difficult. If you want to use the space below, bracing can be with shorter struts arranged at the tops of the legs. Plywood gussets inside are simple (Fig. 8-9B). If they are outside as well, the edges should be protected with glue or wood strips to prevent entry of water. Better stiffening is with diagonal struts (Fig. 8-9C). The longer they are, the more effective they will be, but you will have to compromise if you need clearance for access. Even shorter struts can provide good stiffening due to their triangulating effect.

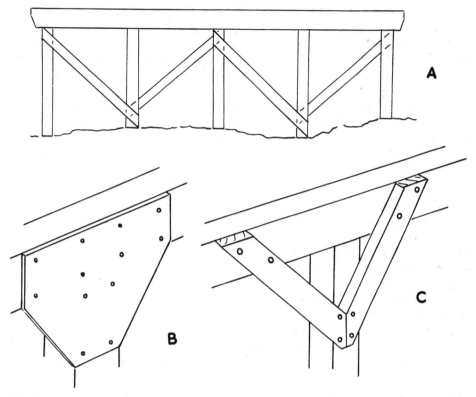

Fig. 8-9. Bracing is needed if the deck supporting posts are high.

DECK STAIRWAY

Stairs are often needed between a deck and the ground or with another level of deck or the house. They have to be planned so steps taken are the same all the way from ground level to the deck level. Having a higher or lower step at an end could cause the user to falter and have an accident. It is usual for the rise of stairs to be no more than 8 inches. If you measure the total height between surfaces, you can divide that into the nearest rise under 8 inches. The amount one step projects ahead of the one above is its *run* (Fig. 8-10A) and this is best if it is more than the *rise*. Shallower rises usually have wider runs. With a rise of 8 inches, the run might be 9 inches. If the rise is only 7 inches, the run would be better 10 inches or 11 inches.

Obviously you have to adapt to the available space. You cannot do anything about the total height, but you could make one more or less riser. Adjust the spread of the stair to fit within the available space. Most stairways are a compromise, but for ease of use aim at the suggested relation between rise and run. The angle of a stairway is flatter than 45 degrees to horizontal, and that must be allowed for (it extends more than it rises).

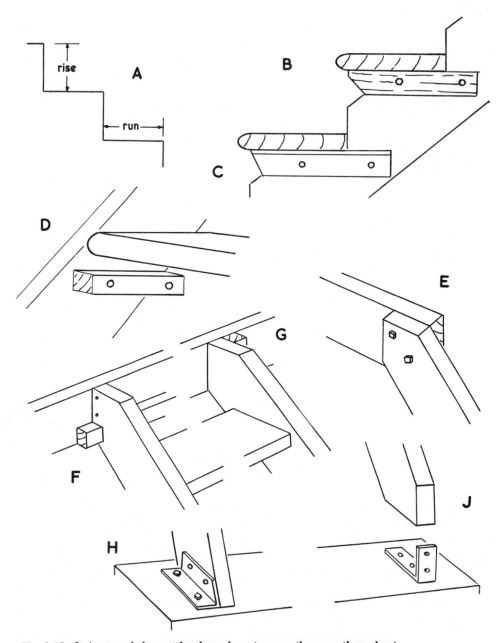

Fig. 8-10. Stairs to a deck must be planned so steps are the same throughout.

The two side supports are called stringers and they can support the treads in several ways. Because of the stringer angle in relation to the tread widths, they have to be fairly wide—usually 2 inches thick and 10 inches or 12 inches wide.

Treads are best as wide as the run, or a little more, but some stairways have the rear edge of each tread slightly forward of the nose of the one above. Stair widths are usually between 24 inches and 36 inches, and can have treads 2 inches thick.

1. It is possible to partially notch treads into stringers and support them with wood cleats securely bolted on (Fig. 8-10B). There could be steel angle instead of wood cleats (Fig. 8-10C). Notching treads into dadoes, as is often done on indoor stairways, is not recommended for exterior work. If the treads are to come wholly within the stringers, they are better on bolted cleats. (Fig. 8-10D).

2. At the top, the stringers must be secured to the decking. If there are joists at convenient spacings, they can be bolted through (Fig. 8-10E). The stringers could be notched over ledgers and toe nailed (Fig. 8-10F), but there would be less obstruction to feet with cleats outside (Fig. 8-10G).

3. If the foot of the stairway is at ground level, it should be a concrete pad to avoid rot. The stringers could have cleats or steel angle outside, with anchor bolts set in the concrete (Fig. 8-10H). Another way to take any thrust uses stout strip iron bolted down and the wood stringers fit into the bends (Fig. 8-10J)

4. A stairway could go off the deck squarely at any point. Usually the deck boards are carried out on extended joists (Fig. 8-11A). If the boards are met end on, they should be cut back over a piece added inside and a cover strip fitted (Fig. 8-11B).

5. It might be more convenient to have the stairs alongside the deck. In that case, the joists have to be extended to take boards to form a landing (Fig. 8-11C). In most constructions, this can be allowed to cantilevers from the deck—providing the extension is no more than 30 inches—but there will have to be another post at the corner.

6. Less commonly, the stairway top can be set back into the deck. If the cutout is much, there are problems of support and railings will have to be arranged around the top for safety.

7. A stairway of just a few treads can be safe without a hand rail, but in most cases there have to be railings or bannisters. Construction can be the same as for the deck. This will give a uniform and attractive appearance.

8. Bolt the rail posts to the outsides of the stringer (Fig. 8-11D). Attach rails to them in the same way as around the deck (Fig. 8-11E). Maintain a similar height above the treads so that anyone using the stairway and the edge of the deck will not have to change the height of their grip.

9. How close you arrange the posts depends on your needs. Posts opposite every tread will give a balluster effect, but placing them at every second or third step—with a rail parallel with the stringer lower down—will provide ample protection.

DECK SEATS

Sets of various sorts are the commonest furniture used on a deck. They could be loose chairs, benches, loungers, and other portable things, but permanent bench seats around the sides of the deck have at least two advantages. They are always there for use, without having to carry seating from elsewhere, and they can strengthen the structure if built in when the deck is made. Of course, it is always possible to add benches inside railings on an existing deck, but when they

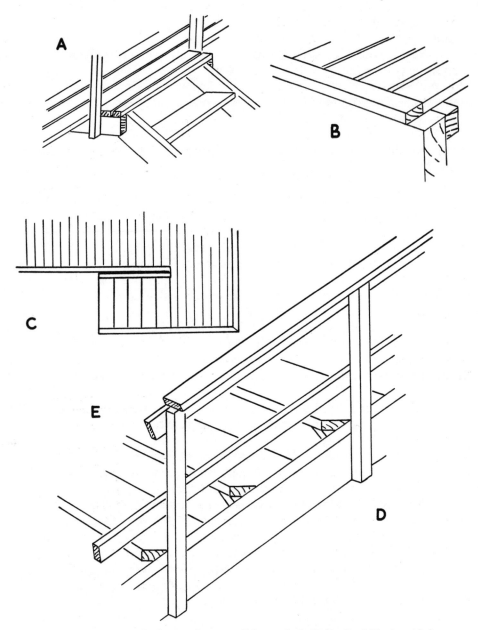

Fig. 8-11. A stairway can lead squarely or parallel to a deck. Rails should be provided.

are made at the same time as the deck it is possible to bond them to the structure so they become part of it. Bench seats inside the railings fit into the whole visual effect and are an added attraction (Fig. 8-13).

Seating is best planned and made *after* the joists have been fitted and *before* the deck boards and railing posts have been fitted, this allows the seat parts to

Fig. 8-12. *A stairway and its rails should be firmly bedded on a concrete base.*

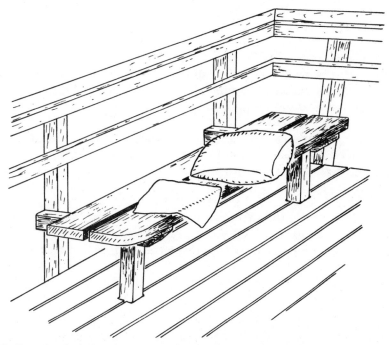

Fig. 8-13. *Seats inside deck railings can contribute to strength.*

become structural members instead of additions. If seats are to extend only partially along a side, you have to allow for the line of railings to match where they are open and where they form seat backs. In most situations, allow for the fronts of the seats to be about 15 inches above the finished deck. If the capping of the railing is between 30 inches and 36 inches above the deck, that will be satisfactory for both a barrier when standing and a seat back.

1. The railing posts will have to be upright to suit places where there are no seats, but a seat is more comfortable with a slight slope. Posts to joist ends can be attached at a slight angle (Fig. 8-14A); 10 degrees should be satisfactory. If the posts are to attach to the sides of joists or beams, they will have to beveled. They can be reduced at the top for neatness (Fig. 8-14B).

2. Where the seat will be square to the joists, front supports can be taken through and bolted to them (Fig. 8-14C). The same spacing as the railing posts should do, but 60 inches is about the maximum for a seat to be stiff between supports (depending on its material).

3. Where the seat will be in line with the joists, the front supports could be on top of the deck boards. For strength they are better taken through to pieces put between the joists (Fig. 8-14D).

4. The seat top could be level, but it is more comfortable if it slops back a little. Making it square to posts sloping at 10 degrees should be about right (Fig. 8-14E). If you want to take the seat around a corner, the slope introduces complications and you might prefer to leave it parallel with the deck.

5. If there are no railings, you could settle for simple benches. In that case, double supports are needed (Fig. 8-14F). Otherwise, construction can be the same as for seats against railings.

6. There is a choice of seat tops. You could join boards to make solid seats; you could use boards similar to those on the deck, or there could be wider boards. Leave narrow gaps (Fig. 8-14G). The seat front should be about 15 inches forward of the strips that form the railings, but the boards need not go fully back.

7. At a corner with a horizontal top, take one seat top through and support the other over a cleat on it (Fig. 8-15A).

8. If the seats slope you cannot do this. Instead, it is better to miter the boards. Have supports as close as you can on each side, and then run the boards over, they need not make a close fit to each other (Fig. 8-15B).

9. If the deck is covered with boards standing on edge, matching seat tops can be made in a similar way (possibly with a 2-inch width and a depth of 3 inches or 4 inches). Use spacers at intervals in the same way as suggested for the low deck. On the seat, the gaps could be wider than on the deck; up to ¾ of an inch is reasonable (Fig. 8-15C). At a corner of a seat laid horizontally, you can get an interesting effect by overlapping alternate strips (Fig 8-15D).

10. Consider how the decking will be laid. Where the seat supports are bolted to joists, it is convenient to arrange them symmetrically in a space (Fig. 8-15E). If much has to come out of a deck board, nail on a cleat below to support it. Where the supports are on pieces between joists, they can be adjusted in the preliminary layout so they come in gaps and little has to be cut away (Fig. 8-15F). If much has to be removed from a board, put a supporting cleat below.

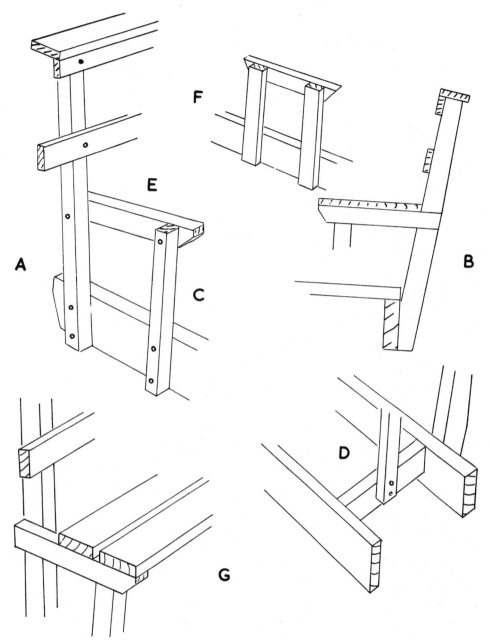

Fig. 8-14. Constructional details of deck seats.

WALKWAY

A boardwalk or raised walkway can be made like a deck, but usually it will be simpler. As it is narrower than a deck, there is no need for joists on beams in most cases. The posts that support the decking can continue up to form railing posts. Any length is possible, but in most gardens the assembly is more likely

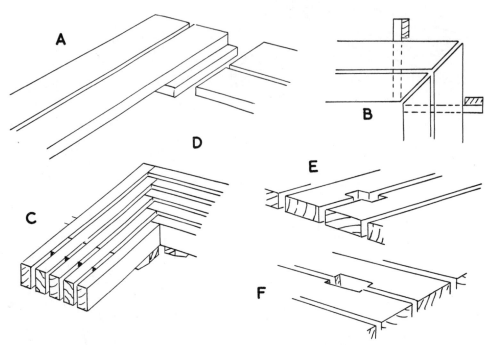

Fig. 8-15. Seats can be made with flat or edge boards and joined at the corners.

Fig. 8-16. A walkway can be made in the same way as a deck.

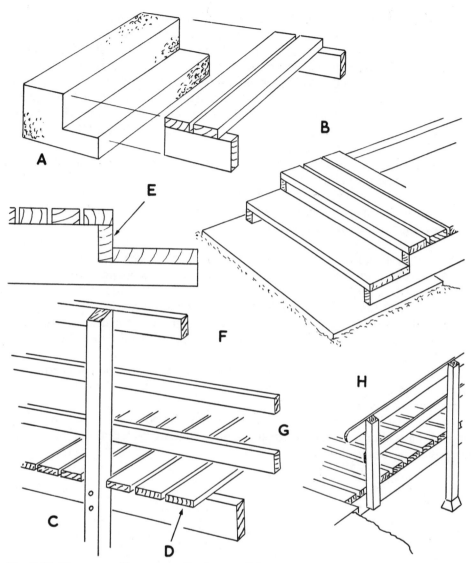

Fig. 8-17. The posts will support rails. Steps will be needed.

to be fairly short to cover a ditch, an uneven patch, or marshy ground. In many situations the walkway might even be regarded as a bridge. Figure 8-16 shows such a walkway, but the same methods could be used for much longer structures.

It is assumed that the walkway crosses a hollow and a pair of posts to the ground are used. They can be 3 inches square for most structures. If the span between them is not more than 7 feet, the joists could be 8 inches deep and 2 inches wide. You can have 2-inch-thick boards forming the decking if the joists are not more 36 inches apart. Railings can be similar to those already suggested for decks, but the extended posts will provide support.

1. Use strings to lay out the two sides. Decide on the way you will treat the ends. If you want to take anything with wheels across, the approach should be level. The joists could fit into concrete blocks (Fig. 8-17A) that are arranged so the top of the concrete and the deck level will match the approach surface. If it is not important that the deck be level, you could rest the joists on flat concrete pads and make two shallow wide steps. The total height of 10 inches is too much for a single step, but you can cut the ends of the joists to take one wide tread midway between the surface level and the top of the deck boards (Fig. 8-17B).

2. The joists in position can be used to locate the posts. Check that they are level and parallel, and that there is no twist when you view from one side.

3. Make the posts long enough to extend about 36 inches above the deck level. The bottoms can be treated and driven into the ground, but they will be better set in concrete or on concrete pads as described earlier in this chapter. Check that they are vertical and bolt them to the joists (Fig. 8-17C).

4. Lay the decking strips across the joists; use 1-inch gaps. The strips need not be cut level, but they should extend an inch or so each side (Fig. 8-17D).

5. At each end, if there is a step, put a piece across between the joists to support the deck strip. The strips will then receive most loads and wear (Fig. 8-17E). You will find this also advisable with a level approach.

6. Bolt or screw on top rails (Fig. 8-17F). The can extend a little at each end. There could be a capping strip on the rails but if not, slope the top of the posts to shed rainwater.

7. One lower rail might be enough, but it will probably be better to have two rails that are evenly spaced (Fig. 8-17G) or closer to the deck if you want to prevent wheels from running over the edge.

8. If the walkway has to be arranged so that the posts are some way from the end, have short railing posts near the ends that are bolted to the joists, but not projecting below them (Fig. 8-17H).

9
CHAPTER

Concrete and Masonry

Stone blends with soil and vegetation in a garden to keep a natural appearance, and can be used to break up the mass of flowers and leaves with a solid, more somber contrast. Stones can also be used structurally for walls and other constructions. If a garden is to be broken into different levels, stone walls are often the most attractive way of retaining and supporting higher levels.

There are now many manufactured substitutes for natural stone. The regular shapes and sizes make assembly easier, but the effect will be a more formal appearance. Perhaps that is what you want. Precast concrete blocks with decorative surfaces or piercings can make a suitable surround for a patio or divisions in a garden, possibly between a formal layout and a more natural one.

Bricks are more traditional than precast blocks. Bricks with color and texture give a more earthy and natural look than those used in houses. Nevertheless, that type of brick would be appropriate if you are making a wall or other structure near the house.

Concrete can be regarded as stone that you can shape and it will hold that form and be structurally storing. The finished thing will still be concrete and will never fool the viewer into believing it is stone, but concrete has many uses in a garden or yard.

MIXING CONCRETE

The active part of concrete is cement that is usually bought in bags. It must be kept dry until it is used. Sand should be free of soil and other impurities, and should also be dry. Because sand is usually stored outdoors and will have absorbed moisture from the air, you might have to use it while it is damp. Avoid sand that is saturated because it will not mix properly and the result will be weak concrete.

195

Aggregate is another name for gravel and stones. The stones can be anything from not much more than sand size up to an inch or so across. The aggregate should be clean and dry.

The proportions can be varied according to the intended use. For much garden concrete work, you can be wide of the theoretical ratios and still achieve satisfactory results. Aim to get them right. An easy to remember proportion is 1:2:3 (1 of cement, 2 of sand and 3 of aggregate). For foundations the amount of aggregate is increased. If it is mortar you are making, where there will not be aggregate; 1 of cement to 3 or 4 of sand will do. There are theoretical proportions of water to be added, but this is difficult to assess because the sand may already contain water. It is more usual to rely on the appearance of the mix.

If there is much concrete to be mixed, it will be advisable to rent a power-driven mixer. If the site is accessible to a truck, you might prefer to take a delivery of ready-mixed concrete, remember to get your quantity right as most suppliers will not want to take away unwanted mixture.

If all you want is a small amount, work on a clean surface. A piece of plywood is suitable. Put down the sand and aggregate and add the cement. Then very thoroughly mix dry with a spade. This is important. Spray on a little water and mix again. You could pour some water into a hollow at the center. Mix by turning over the spade.

After working in that water, add more and mix again, usually by lifting the outside and turning into the center. For such purposes as postholes, aim to get the mixture wet right through, but barely pourable. When you work the spade up and down in it, the concrete mixture should be plastic and stay in the ridges you make. Wiping over with the flat of the spade should leave a smooth surface. Use the mixture within an hour or so (depending on the conditions). If the heat of the sun makes water evaporate rapidly, you will have to work more quickly.

LAYING CONCRETE

If you are laying foundations or filling a posthole, there can be stones and gravel in the bottom, rammed down. Then the concrete can be poured and shoveled in. Tamp it with the spade or shovel edges and perhaps ram it with the end of a piece of post so that air is excluded.

You can build up the bulk in a foundation with larger stones, but make sure they are clean and wet them as you bury them in the concrete. If it is a post you are laying concrete around, support it and ram the concrete around it. Then use a flat trowel to smooth the surface to a slightly conical form at the top (Fig. 9-1A). A raised top can be shaped with a simple form made from boards (Fig. 8-4F). The boards can be pulled away after the concrete has set.

It is possible to make a slab away from where it will be used, but in most gardens it will be simpler and better to cast it in position. If the concrete is to be walked on, it should be about 2 inches or more thick over a firm foundation of stones and gravel. Dig out and make a frame of boards with straight tops held in place with pegs (Fig. 9-1B). Check that the tops are horizontal. If the slab is to be rectangular, check squareness by measuring diagonals. An inaccurate shape

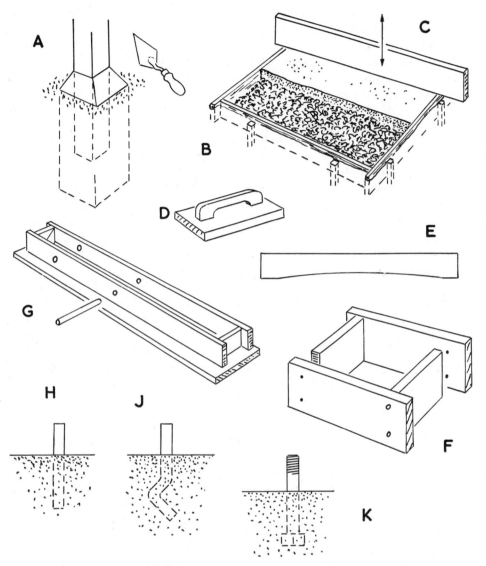

Fig. 9-1. *Much concrete work involves wooden forms and tools. Pegs and bolts can be set into the concrete.*

will be rather obvious. Ram stones and gravel into the bottom; leave enough depth above for the concrete. Lightly water the stones just before pouring the concrete. Otherwise too much moisture will be drawn out of the concrete too soon.

Use a straight board on edge to level the surface of the concrete (Fig. 9-1C). At first, this can be bounced up and down as it is moved along slowly. That leaves a generally level surface but with small ridges. Such a surface gives a good foot grip. If you want a smooth surface, go over with sweeps of a float made from a flat piece of wood and a handle (Fig. 9-1D).

A path can be made in the same way as a slab, but it is inadvisable to attempt a very long length in one operation. Prepare the form boards for the whole length and put in the stones of the base. Then divide the path into convenient lengths (about 6 feet). Put pieces across and lay alternate bays. When they have set, remove the dividing boards and lay concrete in the spaces between. A path can be flat, but there is an advantage in giving it a slight camber or crown so that water runs off to the sides. Plane a board to the curve you want and use that on the surface (Fig. 9-1E).

If you want to make concrete blocks or slabs of a size that can be handled, make simple forms with two angles (Fig. 9-1F). Use nails or screws so they can be taken apart. There are nails with twin heads for this purpose.

With the form on a smooth surface, you can put in the concrete and level the top. After a few hours, the block will have set hard enough for the form to be opened carefully and removed, and ready for use again. Items of other shapes can be cast in this way. Much depends on your ingenuity in making forms. Remember that the form has to be tapered so it will pull away or it must be suitable for disassembly.

Concrete posts can be made in forms with dowels through to form bolt holes (Fig. 9-1G). Remove the dowels before the concrete has fully hardened.

For the attachment of wood, you will have to set in spikes or bolts. A plywood template duplicating the holes in the wood is useful as an indication of positions. A simple spike will give locations (Fig. 9-1H), but it could pull out. It is better with a few bends (Fig. 9-1J). A bolt head buried deep enough will provide its own security (Fig. 9-1K). When to put in the metal depends on the mix. If it is rather runny, let it begin to harden, and then put in the metal and trowel around it.If it is a thick, barely plastic mix, you can put the bolt or spike in as you level the top.

Concrete is strongest if it does not dry too quickly. In moderate temperatures, it can just be left. Wet burlap laid over it will delay drying in hot or windy conditions. It must not be allowed to freeze before it has set; cover it when frost is expected.

STONE AND BRICK PATHS

A supply of flat stones or bricks can be used to make a path. Estimate your needs carefully because a surprising number are needed to go very far. Isolated stones of interesting shapes can be used like stepping stones in a lawn. Very little preparation is required.

Paths are often "crazy paved" with stones of irregular shapes. Unfortunately, you need many stones to fit into each other because gaps must not be very large. Such a path needs fairly straight edges. A temporary margin of board can be used to indicate width and height. Unless the soil is very firm, use a base of gravel. Over this can come sand only or a sand and cement mix that will grip the stones and discourage weeds growing between them (Fig. 9-2A). You could use this mortar between the stones as well, but open gaps, or those filled with soil, are usually preferred.

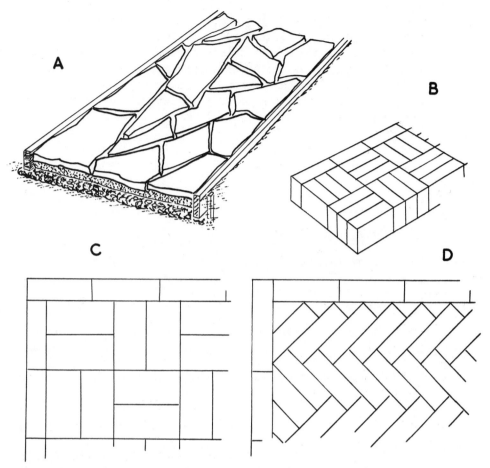

Fig. 9-2. Stone and brick paths can be set in patterns.

If you have to cut stones, the correct tool is a wide chisel sometimes called a *bolster*. You can use an engineer's cold chisel. To bed the stones down and level them, a heavy log bounced up and down is better than a hammer that might break the stones.

Bricks can be laid in a similar way to stones. There are many possibilities for various patterns (Fig. 9-2B, C and D). Mortar can be placed under the bricks and allowed to come almost to surface, which is usual, or allowed to come right to the surface to be troweled level.

Stone or brick paths do not have to be straight. There is an attraction about a slightly winding path or those that broaden in suitable places. It is not so easy to give a crown or camber to these paths, but a board with a suitable curve can be laid across as a guide as the parts are laid.

10
CHAPTER

Buildings

You can store tools and equipment in lockers or other small containers, but in many gardens there is a need for a small building for storage or for use as a greenhouse. It might be possible to build a shed on the side of a house or against a fence, but in many cases it will have to be a freestanding structure. Building such a shed or greenhouse need not be very complicated, and you do not have all the restrictions that come with building a house. The structure can range from a simple shelter made from available material to a well-finished structure that looks like a smaller counterpart of your house.

Construction is usually of wood, but walls could be partially or completely made of bricks or precast blocks with wood above. It is not usually necessary to include insulation in walls or roofs, and many sheds have nothing in the walls except the sheathing that is visible outside. Roofs can be treated in a similar way, but they can include two or more layers to ensure weatherproofing.

A fairly large building will have to be built in position, but for sheds of a size often needed in a garden, prefabricated panels can be bolted together on the site. This means you can make the parts in your shop or elsewhere (perhaps when the weather is unsuitable for work outside). It also allows you to take a building apart and move it to another position with minimum trouble.

PLAYHOUSE/SHED

If you have space to build a playhouse, your children will get a lot of satisfaction out of using it, but children grow up and you can reach a stage where a building that is just a playhouse has no further use. If it is a scaled-down size, there is not much you can do with it. If there is space, it is better to start with a building that can have other uses. That means it should be large enough for adult use. Children will quite happily play in it.

The building shown in Fig. 10-1 has an enclosed part large enough for most adults to stand in and a porch area large enough for them to sit in. The whole thing gives plenty of scope for several children to use. The back is a large lift-out door. Quite large garden equipment can be put inside for storage, and that end might be used for access even when children are playing at the other end.

The suggested sizes (Fig. 10-2A) allow for cutting plywood sheets with the minimum waste, but covering could be with wood siding or any other means suggested at the beginning of the chapter. The enclosed area is about 7 feet by 8 feet, and this gets natural light through windows at one or both sides and in the front door. The porch extends 5 feet and can have fixed side benches ,or there is ample space for several chairs. A wood floor is shown, but the building could go on a concrete slab.

Modifications are easy at the planning stage. Check on available space and compare access and sitting arrangements to see that they are feasible if you intend very different sizes.

1. The key part is the central partition (Fig. 10-2B). Other parts have to be matched to it; make it first. Most of the wood is 2 inch × 4 inch. Check the actual dimensions; they could be undersize. There are five lengthwise pieces that should go right through from one end of the building to the other (without joins if

Fig. 10-1. Front of a playhouse/shed.

possible). There is a ridge (Fig. 10-2C) and two eaves (Fig. 10-2D), with other pieces at the side (Fig. 10-2E) and foot (Fig. 10-2F). They could be notched fully into the uprights, but it is better to cut a small amount (⅝ inch is suitable, out of the long piece and more out of the upright (Fig. 10-3A). At the ridge, nail the rafters against the lengthwise piece (Fig. 10-3B). Include a central upright piece over the door.

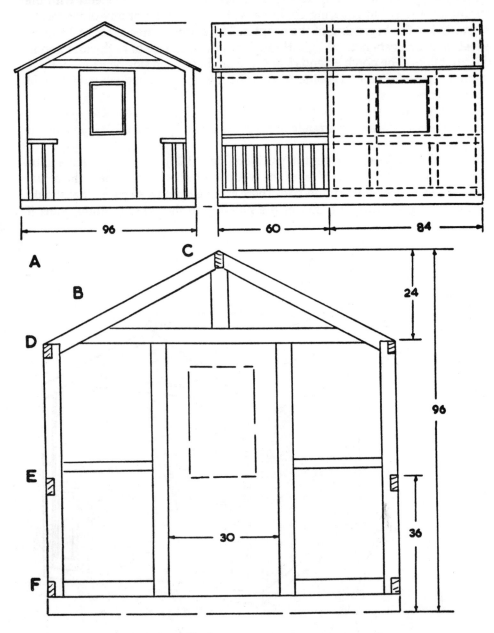

Fig. 10-2. Sizes of the playhouse/shed.

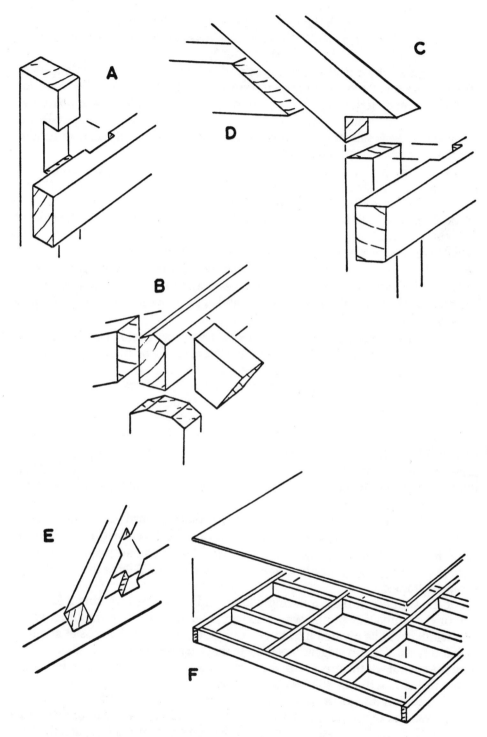

Fig. 10-3. Details of the framing and floor of the playhouse/shed.

2. At the eaves, notch the lengthwise piece into the upright. Then arrange the rafter to fit over (Fig. 10-3C). The piece across above the door should have its underside level with the eaves (Fig. 10-3D). Nail it to the rafter.

3. With all the partition parts prepared, assemble them on two sheets of plywood that meet over the central upright. it is advisable to use plywood for this partition even if the outside is to be covered with shiplap or other boarding. Assemble with glue and nails. Be careful to keep the doorway sides parallel. If the plywood needs stiffening, put pieces across the side panels at half door height. Use this assembly as a pattern for making other parts.

4. For the back of the shed, make an assembly to the same overlap sizes as the partition. Alter the door opening to almost full width (Fig. 10-4D). Unless absolutely you need the maximum door width to get your equipment in, it is advisable to have a little width left on each side of the doorway for the sake of stiffness.

5. For the front of the porch, allow for strips forming the outline. You can arrange the horizontal piece higher than in the partition for more headroom (Fig. 10-4B), and it can overlap the inner surfaces of the rafters. Even if you will not be fitting side benches, it helps in stiffness and appearance if there is some framing on each side.

6. Install a truss midway along the enclosed part. That is like the top part of the partition framing, but the horizontal piece could be higher (Fig. 10-4C). It can overlap the rafters instead of meeting at the edges.

7. There will have to be some preparation of the rafters to suit the chosen roof covering. If you are using ½ inch, exterior-plywood or particleboard it might have sufficient stiffness, but it is advisable to use at least one lengthwise purlin midway between the ridge and eaves. That can be 2-inch ×-2-inch strip notched in (Fig. 10-3E). If you have to make up lengths, do that in a joint. If there are to be shingles or other coverings, space purlins to suit. If you need a large number, they could go on the surfaces of the rafters, but you would have to cover their ends later.

8. If the floor is to be framed plywood or particleboard, make that next. If you build it in one piece, it will probably have to be assembled in position. It could be in sections, all full width, but one for the porch and two for the other part. A one-piece floor is easier to keep flat and in shape. There are several ways it can be framed.

For the stiffness of most covering you should not exceed framing 2 feet by 2 feet or the equivalent (if one way is longer, make it narrower the other way). The width could be divided into three, and then pieces fitted across at about 18 inch intervals. You can stagger meetings to make nailing easier (Fig. 10-3F). Make sure the overall width agrees with the partition and its matching parts, but slight errors in the length can still be allowed for.

9. Position the floor and mount the partition and back on it. Check squareness and temporarily nail these parts in position. Put the long side strips (Fig. 10-2D, E and F) in position. See that the main parts are upright, steady them with temporary diagonal struts. Add the other uprights to the sides of the closed

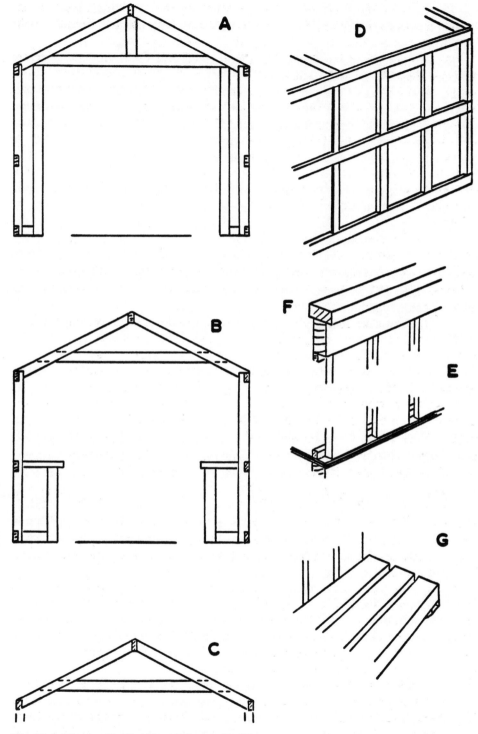

Fig. 10-4. Trusses (A-C), sides, and seats (D-G).

part and frame around where the windows will come (Figs. 10-4D and 10-5A). Fit the plywood or other skin to the sides of the building, this will hold the main parts in shape.

10. Fit the truss to the closed part (Figs. 10-4C and 10-5B) and the porch at the front (Figs. 10-4B and 10-5C). Put the ridge (Fig. 10-2C) in place.

11. At the sides of the porch, there can be plywood closing the lower part or you can arrange palings between the long strips (Fig. 10-4E). Arrange the top piece (Fig. 10-4F) with rounded edges along the rail. This can be continued about 18 inches around the front (Fig. 10-2A) whether you want to fit bench seats at the side or not. Bench seats are simply made with strips on end supports (Fig. 10-4G).

12. Cover the roof with shingles. At the porch there could be a decorative barge board (Fig. 10-5D).

13. The window can be framed around and glazed in the same way as described for the previous project.

14. The front door could be ledged and braced as in the previous project, but another way to make it is to use two pieces of plywood—with framing between (Fig. 10-6A). Make sure there is solid wood where the hinges, lock, and window come together. The plywood edges can be left exposed or covered with thin strips. Frame around for the window and hold the glass in with strips (Fig. 10-6B).

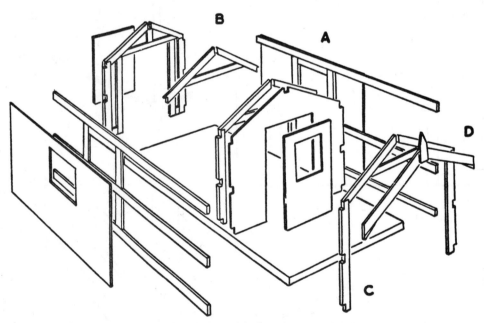

Fig. 10-5. The subassemblies of the playhouse/shed.

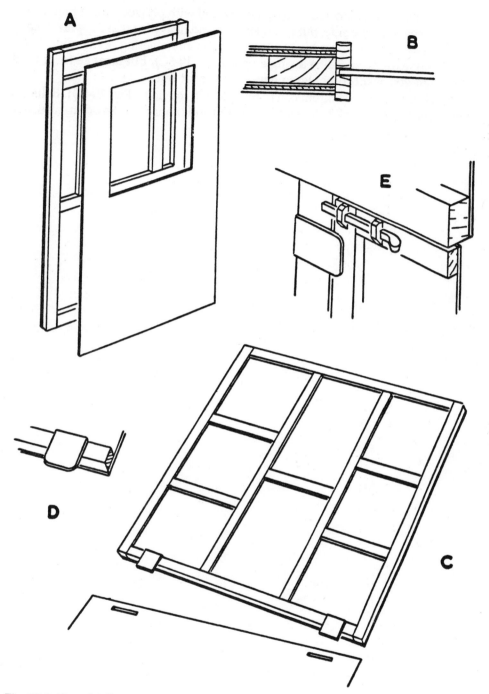

Fig. 10-6. Door details.

15. The back door could be a frame covered with plywood or shiplap boards as then hinged at one side, but is rather wide and heavy for that support. It could be made as a pair of doors hinged at both sides and meeting at the middle. Another way is to make it like a single door (Fig. 10-6C), but arrange for it to lift out when you want to get large equipment in or out.

Projections on the bottom can fit into slots in the floor (Fig. 10-6D). Bolts and a stop inside the top will hold it up (Fig. 10-6E) and cannot be opened from outside.

Glossary

The making of outdoor tools and equipment forms only part of the crafts of woodworking and metalworking. The selection of words that follows are some that are particularly appropriate to the subjects of this book, and may be helpful to readers unfamiliar with the language of craftwork.

aggregate—Stone, gravel, or sand used with cement to make concrete.

alloy—A substance composed of one or more chemical elements, at least one of which is metal. Brass is an alloy of copper and zinc.

anchor bolt—A bolt set in concrete with its threaded end projecting.

annealing—Softening metal. Steel is annealed by being heated to redness and cooled slowly.

apex—The top or peak of a roof.

backfill—To fill an excavation around a post or foundation.

barrel bolt—A sliding door fastener.

batten—A narrow strip of wood.

beam—A horizontal, load-bearing structural member.

blind—Not right through, such as a stopped hole.

brazing—Joining parts by flowing a thin layer of nonferrous filler metal in the space between them. This is oridinarily done at temperatures above 800 degrees F. At lower temperatures the process is called soldering.

bridging—Wood fitted between joists to spread load.

butt—End to end.

carriage bolt—A bolt with a shallow round head and a square neck.

cast—1.(v) To pour metal or concrete into a mold. 2.(n) Twisting of a surface that should be flat.

cement—Fine powder, which is the active ingredient of concrete when mixed with sand and stones with water.

check—A split in wood in the direction of grain.

cleat—A strip of wood used as a support or a brace across other wood.

clench(clinch)—To turn over the extending end of a nail.

concrete—A mixture of sand, cement, aggregate, and water.

conversion—The general term for cutting a log into boards and smaller pieces of wood for use.

counterbore—To let the head of a screw or bolt below surface.

countersink—To set the screw or bolt head level with the surface.

course—A row of stones, bricks, or shingles.

dado—A groove cut across the grain of a board.

dead pin—A wedge or dowel.

drift—A tapered punch used to drive through holes to bring them in line.

eaves—An overhang of roof over wall or an angle between them.

feather edge—The thinned edge of a piece of wood.

ferrule—A metal tube at end of handle to reduce risk of splitting when a tool tang is driven in.

float—A flat wood tool for smoothing surface of concrete.

footing—Masonry or concrete form to support wall.

foundation—A support in the ground for a structure.

foxiness—The sign of the first onset of wood rot.

frost line—Depth frost is expected to penetrate into soil.

gable—The vertical end of a building with inverted V end of roof.

galvanized iron—Iron or mild steel coated with zinc as protection against rust.

girder—Wood or metal beam.

glazing—A glass pane, the fitting of a glass pane.

glazing compound—Sealing and glass-setting compound as alternative to traditional putty.

grade—A slope (gradient).

grout—Thin mortar to pour into cracks.

gusset—A wood or metal joint cover.

haft—A long handle of hammer or similar tool.

handed—Made as a pair.

hardware cloth—A woven steel mesh.

jamb—The side or head lining of window or door.

joggle—Offset double bend in a strip of metal.

kerf—A slot made by a saw.

lag screw—A large wood screw with the head for a wrench.

laying out—Setting out the details of design and construction.

ledger—A strip of wood fitted in position to support board ends.

level (spirit level)—An instrument to determine horizontal direction.

lintel—Support for a load over an opening.

mild steel—Iron with a small amount of carbon content.

mortar—Sand, cement, and water mixture used to bond bricks and stones.

particleboard—A board made by bonding wood chips with synthetic resin.

pegging—Dowels or wood pegs through joints.

pier—A masonry column.

pilot hole—A small hole used as the guide for a drill point when making a larger hole.

pitch—The slope of a roof, the distance between tops of a screw thread.

quartered (quartered sawn)—A board cut radially from a log.

rabbet(rebate)—An angular notch in the side of a piece of wood, as letting in glass.
rail—A horizontal framing member.
retaining wall—A supporting wall subject to lateral pressure.
riddle—A sand or soil sifter.
ridge—Top or apex of roof where sloping sides meet.
rive—To split wood.
roll roofing—Roof covering consisting of felt impregnated with asphalt.
run—Lumber quantity can be described as so many feet run.

sash—A frame containing a pane of glass.
screw—A screw for wood has a tapered thread, but a bolt with its thread almost to the head is also a screw.
seasoning—Drying out wood to an acceptable low level of sap.
shake—A natural crack in wood that develops in the tree.
shank—A neck or part of a tool between the handle and the blade.
sheathing—A covering such as plywood over a frame.
shiplap—Boards which are rabeted to fit into each other.
siding—Covering for the outside of a framed structure.
sill—The lowest member of a frame construction or of an opening.
slat—A narrow, thin wood.
span—The distance between supports.
splay—To spred.
spud—A chisel-like tool for removing bark.
square—Besides an equal-sided rectangle, this also means corners at 90 degrees.
steel—Iron alloyed with carbon. With the correct proportions it can be hardened and tempered.
stringer—Support for cross members, as at the sides of stairs.
stud—Vertical support in a wall.

tang—The tapered end of a tool, such as a file or chisel, to fit into a handle.
template (templet)—The pattern to be used to check or mark pieces to be cut or drilled.
tines—Prongs, as in a fork.
toe nailing—Nailing diagonally where the end of one piece of wood meets another.
tongue and groove—Board edges meeting with a projection on one fitting a groove in the other.
truss—Structural members joined to provide strength and shape, as in a roof truss.

vent—An arrangement in a wall or roof to allow air to flow through.

waney—Edge of board showing the shape of the outside of a log.
warping—Going out of shape as wood dries.
winding—A board twisting in its length.

Index